The Professional Edge Playbook

Five Proven Pillars for Career Mastery

Hani Alkhoudary, Ph.D., APMG-CMP, PMP

ISBN (eBook): 978-1-968563-68-4

ISBN (Paperback): 978-1-968563-69-1

ISBN (Hardcover): 978-1-968563-70-7

Dedication

To my parents, Dr. Mohammed and Mrs. Wejdan.

Your faith in me gave me the courage to dream without limits.

To my wife, Ghadeer.

Your strength and patience have carried me through every challenge and lifted me through every success.

To my children, Mohammed, Hala, Wejdan, Omar, and Mohab.

You remind me every day why excellence matters and why I must keep moving forward.

To my sisters, Lama, Dr. May, and Alaa, and to my brother, Dr. Ahmad.

Your belief in me has never faded, and your support has never failed.

This book is a reminder that greatness begins at home.

And because of you, I never stopped reaching higher.

Foreword

Today's workplace never stands still. Technology evolves at breakneck speed, hierarchies grow flatter, and teams span continents and time zones. During this turbulence, professionalism is both anchor and compass. It grounds our decisions in integrity and points us toward purposeful growth.

I wrote The Professional Edge Playbook because I have seen, time and again, that career success is rarely a matter of raw talent alone. It is the day-to-day expression of character, competence, and clarity of purpose. Over three decades, I have observed a consistent pattern: professionals who thrive share five deliberate habits.

They project an authentic presence. They communicate with precision and empathy. They pursue learning with unrelenting curiosity. They execute with discipline and a bias for results. They cultivate strategic relationships that amplify their impact. These five habits, what I call the Five Pillars of Professional Excellence, form the architecture of this book.

Every chapter weaves together research, hands-on tools, and stories rooted in real coaching conversations. You will meet "The Aspirant," a composite character whose setbacks and victories echo the challenges most of us face. Reflection prompts invite you to translate ideas into action because professionalism is not proven in theory; it is earned in practice.

I invite you to use this book as a companion rather than a manual, a resource you can revisit and share. May it help you shape a reputation built on trust and a career defined by purposeful contribution.

To your journey of professional excellence,

Dr. Hani Alkhoudary

Introduction

Professional excellence isn't something you stumble upon by chance; it's a journey you design with intention and discipline. Along this path, there are five essential pillars you'll need to build and master. These aren't standalone skills; they form the foundation that supports your reputation, your performance, and the impact you leave on others.

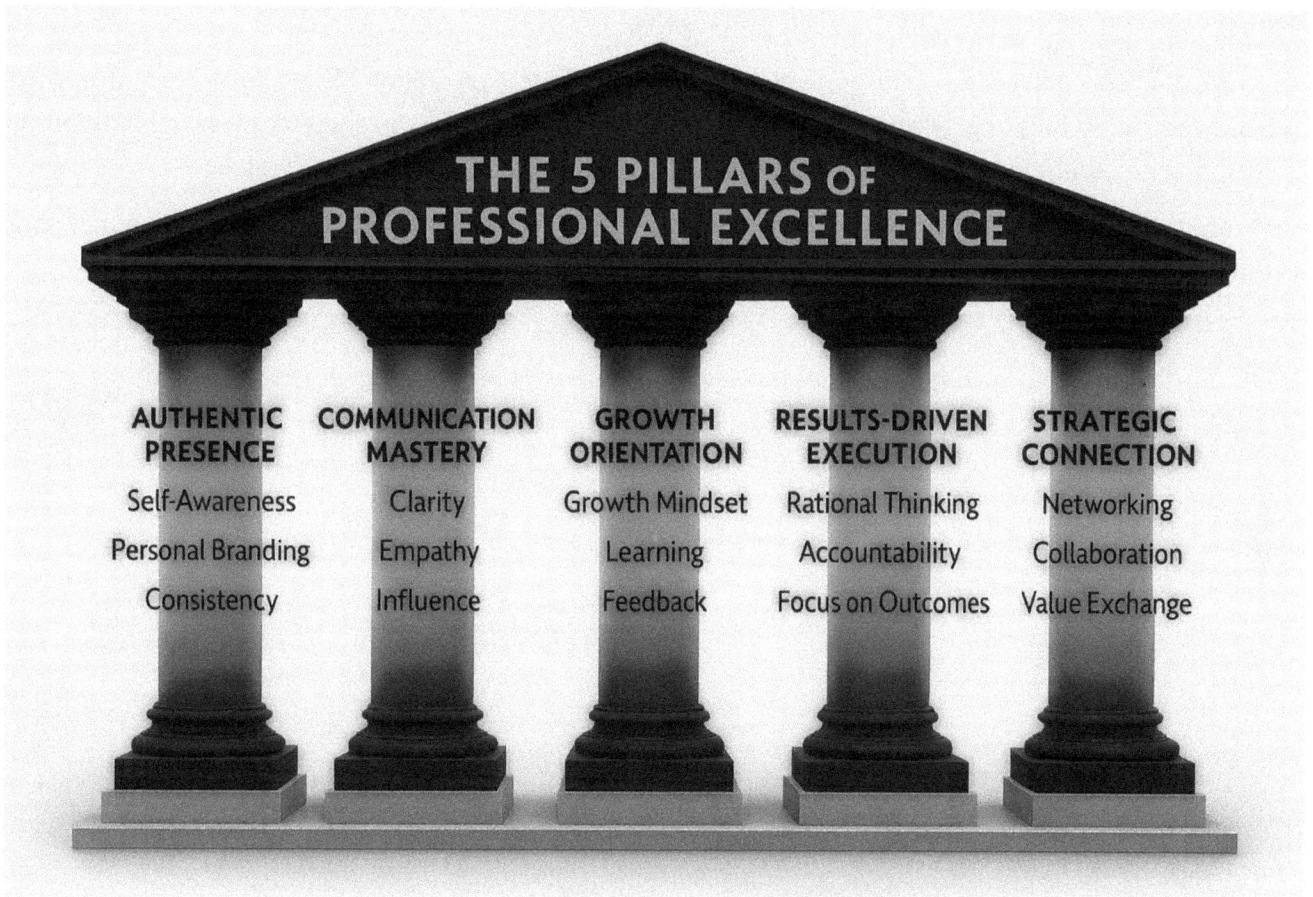

Figure 1: The 5 Pillars of Professional Excellence

Figure 1 depicts these pillars as classical columns holding up the entire structure of excellence itself. Each pillar represents not just a single capability but a set of critical, interdependent strengths that create a durable, integrated framework for success.

Your journey begins with Authentic Presence. This is your compass, the starting point for building trust and credibility. It's about consistently acting with integrity, aligning your personal brand with your values, and becoming known as someone others can count on. You don't just represent yourself; you become a cultural ambassador for your team and organization.

With that trust in place, you develop Communication Mastery. This is your ability to make ideas clear, foster empathy in every exchange, and use influence responsibly. Mastering communication means uniting diverse teams, resolving conflicts before they escalate, and inspiring people to act on shared goals.

The path continues with Growth Orientation, the mindset that ensures you never stagnate. It's your commitment to ongoing learning, seeking feedback, even when it's uncomfortable, and staying adaptable in the face of change. Instead of fearing mistakes, you use them to sharpen your skills and expand your thinking.

As you develop, Results-Driven Execution becomes central. Strategy shifts into action with defined goals and consistent discipline. You measure progress honestly, hold yourself accountable, and ensure that your work delivers tangible, meaningful results.

Finally, you unlock your full potential through Strategic Connection. You move beyond individual achievement by building genuine, reciprocal relationships. This pillar is about networking with purpose, fostering collaboration across silos, and creating value that benefits everyone involved.

These Five Pillars aren't a one-time checklist. They're a framework you'll return to again and again throughout your career. They're how you turn professional promise into proven impact.

How to Use This Book

This book is structured around the Five Pillars of Professional Excellence. Each chapter is designed to help you truly *understand*, *practice*, and *master* one pillar in depth, so you can embed it into your daily work and leadership.

You won't just read about theory. Each chapter includes insights drawn from research and real-world experience, along with practical tools, case studies, and exercises. These resources are designed to help you:

- Build the core competencies of each pillar
- Reflect on your own practice and mindset
- Apply proven strategies to real-world challenges
- Measure your progress and impact

Here's a brief guide to what you'll find in each chapter:

Chapter 1 | Authentic Presence

Trust is the currency of modern work. This chapter will help you define your core values, craft a compelling personal narrative, and align your in-person and digital presence. By the end, you'll have a clear, consistent professional identity that inspires confidence and earns trust.

Chapter 2 | Communication Mastery

Influence is built on the foundations of clarity and empathy. Here you'll learn practical techniques for active listening, concise writing, and intentional body language, skills that transform ordinary interactions into opportunities for leadership.

Chapter 3 | Growth Orientation

Static expertise quickly becomes obsolete. In this chapter, you'll cultivate a growth mindset, design personal learning loops, and turn feedback into fuel. Case studies show how small, consistent curiosity can lead to career-long adaptability.

Chapter 4 | Results-Driven Execution

Ideas only matter if they produce outcomes. You'll learn to set rational priorities, develop execution plans that can handle real-world turbulence, and adopt accountability mechanisms that help you stay focused under pressure.

Chapter 5 | Strategic Connection

No one excels alone. This final chapter reframes networking as a disciplined, values-based practice. You'll map your existing relationships, identify partnership gaps, and learn how to create reciprocal value that lasts far beyond a single project.

This book is your roadmap. Each chapter is a step on the journey toward the kind of professional excellence that isn't just noticed, but respected, trusted, and remembered.

Table of Contents

Chapter One: Authentic Presence

Excellence in any field cannot rest on expertise or talent alone. It must withstand uncertainty, rivalry, and evolving demands. What truly sets remarkable professionals apart is something deeper and more enduring: authentic presence. This is the ability to understand yourself thoroughly, to communicate your identity with clarity, and to show up reliably in ways that inspire trust, establish credibility, and create meaningful impact.

Authentic presence doesn't happen by chance. It is built through deliberate reflection, disciplined practice, and consistent commitment. It gives professionals the grounding to navigate complexity without losing their integrity, to lead teams with purpose, to earn reputations that open doors, and to achieve results that genuinely matter.

At the heart of authentic presence lies self-awareness. Without it, even the best strategies and skills fall short. Self-awareness is more than knowing your personality type or listing your preferences. It's the disciplined, honest, ongoing work of understanding your core values, strengths, motivations, blind spots, and the effect you have on others.

Yet self-awareness alone is not enough. To truly establish an authentic presence, you also need to share who you are in a way that is clear, consistent, and compelling. That is the essence of personal branding. Personal branding is not about self-promotion or projecting an artificial image. It is about deliberately defining your professional identity so that others clearly see the value you offer. The wider industry, along with colleagues, clients, and employers, understands who you are through your values, strengths, experiences, and purpose. Crafting a personal brand means turning internal clarity into an external commitment.

But even a deeply self-aware professional with a strong personal brand can stumble without consistency and engagement. These are the disciplines that turn intention into real, lasting impact. Consistency is the foundation of trust. It means showing up in person, online, in writing, and in meetings in ways that are aligned and dependable. It's about making sure what you say matches what you do so that people know they can rely on you. Consistency touches everything, from how you look to how you speak to how you act. But presence isn't just about being consistent; it's also about being engaged. Engagement is the energy and focus you bring to your professional relationships and to the communities.

Together, these three elements, self-awareness, personal branding, and consistency with engagement, create a roadmap for achieving professional excellence rooted in authenticity. When you follow these practices, your career will grow, and the workplaces around you will become healthier and more honest. It all starts with one honest reflection, one genuine story, and one intentional choice at a time.

Section 1: Self-Awareness: The Foundation of Professional Excellence

Self-awareness stands at the center of today's complex workplace, forming the ground for lasting excellence. Without it, even the most sophisticated strategies, impressive technical skills, or polished communication can collapse under the weight of pressure, misalignment, or unacknowledged blind spots.

But genuine self-awareness is more than just knowing your personality type or ticking off a list of preferences. It's a disciplined, ongoing commitment to examining who you are, how you operate, and why you make the choices you do. It requires an honest examination of your values, strengths, limitations, motivations, and the actual impact you have on the people around you (Eurich, 2018). Cultivating this level of insight takes humility to accept feedback, courage to face discomfort, and dedication to keep learning and growing (Brown, 2018).

Professionals who invest in this kind of self-awareness earn trust, the essential currency of effective leadership, teamwork, and client relationships (Covey, 2006). They're better equipped to handle conflict with empathy and clarity, to communicate with purpose and precision, and to make career decisions that align with what truly matters to them. They develop resilience under pressure because they possess an internal compass that guides them in adapting without compromising their integrity or purpose (Duckworth, 2016).

This section is here to help transform self-awareness from an abstract ideal or one-time personality exercise into a practical, structured discipline you can use every day. It introduces the Self-Discovery Blueprint, a comprehensive framework designed to help you reflect deeply and organize those insights into an actionable plan for professional growth (Eurich, 2018).

The Self-Discovery Blueprint includes five essential dimensions: Clarifying Your Core Values, Assessing Strengths and Growth Areas, Understanding Your Motivations and Drivers, Articulating Your Impact and Contribution, and Capturing Your Learning Reflections. Through this section, you will work with proven frameworks and guided reflections, using real-world examples to build the clarity and confidence to understand yourself, what drives you, and consistently bring your best self to every professional situation.

By dedicating yourself to this work, you ensure your career choices, leadership style, and daily actions aren't left to chance but are intentionally aligned with the professional impact you want to have. Self-awareness becomes not just a private exercise but a visible strength that underpins trust, influence, and enduring success.

The Self-Discovery Blueprint

To make self-awareness actionable, we introduce the Self-Discovery Blueprint, a practical framework designed to help you map, organize, and reflect on the core dimensions of who you are as a professional (See Figure 2).

Much like businesses use strategy canvases to view the big picture on one page (Osterwalder & Pigneur, 2010), this blueprint enables you to capture the essential elements of your professional identity in an organized and holistic way. It is not a one-time exercise but a living document you can revisit as you grow and change.

Figure 2: Self-Discovery Blueprint Canvas

Values	Strengths	Passions	Purpose	Growth Areas
What truly matters to me?	Where do I excel effortlessly?	What activities energise me?	Why do I do what I do?	Which skills must I develop next

1. Clarifying Your Core Values

Your values are the bedrock of your professional identity (Schwartz, 2012). They define what truly matters to you, guiding your decisions, shaping your priorities, and influencing how you respond to challenges, even in times of pressure or uncertainty.

Key Questions to Reflect On:

❖ **What principles am I unwilling to compromise?**

This question addresses the non-negotiables in your professional life, the ethical boundaries you will not cross, even under pressure. It forces you to identify the foundational beliefs that guide your choices when the stakes are high or when it would be easier to cut corners.

By defining these principles, you set clear boundaries for yourself and others. This is less about ideals and more about recognizing the ground you will not give up. For example, you might be unwilling to compromise on honesty, respect, fairness, or confidentiality.

Reflecting on this question ensures you won't be caught off guard in challenging moments. You'll know in advance what you're prepared to say no to, and you'll project integrity that others can see and trust.

❖ **What values do I want to be known for?**

This question prompts you to reflect on your reputation. It's not only what you believe, but how you want others to perceive you professionally. It's about the legacy you're building in the minds of colleagues, clients, and stakeholders.

Values such as integrity, empathy, accountability, innovation, and service communicate what others can expect from you. By clarifying these, you can be intentional about how you present yourself, ensuring that your actions align with and reinforce the desired professional identity.

This reflection also helps you align your brand with your values, so you're not just living them internally, but expressing them in ways that are clear and consistent to others.

❖ **How do my values show up in my daily actions?**

This is the bridge between *belief* and *behavior*. It pushes you to move beyond vague ideals and consider how your values manifest in concrete ways at work.

For example:

- If you value *integrity*, do you speak up when something is wrong, even if it's uncomfortable?
- If you value *collaboration*, do you invite others' ideas and share credit?
- If you value *empathy*, do you listen deeply and adapt to others' needs?

Together, these questions ensure that your values aren't just words on a page. They help you turn abstract ideals into reliable guides for your decisions, your interactions, and your professional reputation.

By answering them, you lay the foundation for authentic, trustworthy, and effective professional behavior, qualities that define excellence in any field.

Example: Answering the Key Questions on Core Values

What principles am I unwilling to compromise?

"I will not compromise honesty and fairness, even under pressure. I believe in telling the truth respectfully, even when it's uncomfortable. I am also committed to treating everyone with respect and dignity, regardless of their role or background. These principles guide my decisions, negotiations, and leadership style."

What values do I want to be known for?

"I want colleagues and clients to know me for integrity, empathy, and accountability. I want to be seen as someone who can be trusted to do the right thing, who listens and understands others' perspectives, and who reliably delivers on commitments. I also value innovation. I want to be known for finding creative solutions to challenges rather than accepting the status quo."

How do my values show up in my daily actions?

"Integrity is evident when I choose transparency in communication, even when it's challenging. I share project risks openly with stakeholders, rather than sugarcoating them. Empathy is present in the way I lead my team; I check in on their well-being, listen without judgment, and adapt to individual needs. Accountability is evident in my follow-through; when I commit to something, I ensure it gets done, and I take responsibility for mistakes when they occur. Innovation appears in my willingness to question existing processes and propose new approaches, encouraging my team to do the same."

By taking these questions seriously, you turn ideals into commitments that influence the choices you make each day. This ensures alignment between what you believe and how you act, making your professional presence credible, consistent, and deeply authentic.

2. Assessing Strengths and Growth Areas

Self-aware professionals don't just know what's on their résumé; they understand what they do well and where they need to grow (Buckingham & Clifton, 2001). This clarity supports better career decisions, fosters trust, and enables deliberate personal and professional development (Eurich, 2018).

The goal is not perfection. The goal is to recognize your assets and your edges, then use them deliberately to keep growing. Below are four key questions to help you get there:

❖ **What do others consistently rely on me for?**

This question helps you identify the real-world value you bring to teams and organizations. It's easy to list generic skills, but what do people count on you for? Is it solving complex problems? Mediating conflict? Clarifying strategy? Managing details others overlook?

Your answer here grounds your strengths in *evidence*. It highlights your unique role and differentiators in a professional context, offering clues about where you can specialize, lead, or mentor others.

Tip: Reflect on feedback you've received in meetings, performance reviews, or even informal conversations.

❖ **What achievements am I most proud of?**

This question asks you to own your wins and to understand *why* they matter to you. Which projects, results, or moments stand out in your memory? Examples like these demonstrate your capabilities while also reflecting your values, your drive, and your working style.

Are you proud of launching a complex project? Navigating a tough negotiation? Building a new team? Each answer offers insight into your core strengths, passions, and leadership style.

Tip: Write down 2–3 specific achievements and note the skills or qualities that made them possible.

❖ **Where do I feel less confident or skilled?**

Professional excellence demands honest humility. This question helps you identify the areas that can hold you back if left unaddressed. It's not about self-criticism, it's about clarity. Are there technical skills you would like to refine? Leadership abilities you want to develop? Communication habits that need refinement?

By naming these areas, you can create a practical development plan, seek mentoring, or take training courses. It also signals to colleagues and leaders that you're committed to growth, not stuck in defensive denial.

Tip: Ask yourself, 'Where do I hesitate most?' Where do I delegate or avoid?

❖ **What feedback have I received?**

Feedback is a mirror for professional development. This question pushes you to move beyond self-perception and consider how others experience you. Formal reviews, informal comments, or even subtle signals (like being repeatedly asked to fix certain issues) all hold valuable insights.

- Have you been praised for your ability to stay calm under pressure?
- Have you heard that you sometimes miss details?
- Did someone thank you for your clear communication, or suggest you be more concise?

Taking feedback seriously demonstrates emotional intelligence and adaptability, both of which are highly valued in any role.

Tip: Review old performance reviews, emails, or mentoring conversations to mine feedback you might have forgotten.

Example: Answering the Key Questions on Key Strengths

Imagine Michel, a mid-level project manager, reflecting on these questions:

What do others rely on me for?

"They count on me to keep projects on track and calm people down when tensions rise. I'm the one who sees the big picture but doesn't miss the details."

What achievements am I most proud of?

"Delivering a complex IT integration three weeks early, with cross-functional teams that didn't trust each other at first."

Where do I feel less confident?

"Presenting to senior executives, I get nervous and sometimes rush my points."

What feedback have I received?

"That I'm an excellent planner, but could be more assertive in meetings."

Michel realizes his strengths lie in planning, stakeholder alignment, and conflict resolution. He also identifies areas for growth, including executive communication and assertiveness. This self-awareness lets him pursue targeted training, practice with mentors, and position himself confidently for future leadership roles.

Assessing strengths and growth areas is not about perfecting yourself overnight. It's about understanding what you bring to the table and making a conscious plan to build on it, so you can be both practical and adaptable in your career.

3. Understanding Your Motivations and Drivers

Self-awareness is not only about knowing what you're good at; it's also about understanding *why* you choose to do what you do. These inner drivers sustain your energy day after day. They also sharpen your focus and hold your commitment steady. Beyond skills, self-awareness involves understanding why you choose the work you do (Pink, 2009). Motivations sustain focus, energy, and commitment, even on difficult days. They're what push you to go the extra mile, navigate challenges, and find meaning in your work, even on the hardest days.

Professionals who understand their motivations can make better career choices, avoid roles that drain them, and seek projects that bring out their best. They also communicate more clearly about what they want, align with like-minded teams, and demonstrate authenticity that builds trust with colleagues and leaders. Below are three key questions designed to help you clarify your core motivations:

❖ **What aspects of my work energize me?**

This question directly addresses the heart of professional engagement. Which tasks make you lose track of time? Which projects leave you feeling excited rather than exhausted? Do you feel energized when brainstorming new ideas, mentoring colleagues, solving customer issues, analyzing data, or leading strategic discussions? By noticing what gives you energy, you uncover clues about your natural fit and potential for sustainable performance.

Tip: Reflect on your last work week. Which moments felt effortless or even fun?

❖ **What types of challenges do I enjoy solving?**

Motivated professionals often gravitate toward certain kinds of challenges. Some love untangling complex technical problems. Others thrive on people-focused challenges like mediating conflict or building alignment. Some enjoy operational puzzles like improving efficiency or managing large-scale change.

This question helps you identify where you're most willing to invest time, creativity, and perseverance, essential for finding roles and projects that maximize both impact and satisfaction.

Tip: Think about a work challenge you couldn't wait to tackle. What made it appealing?

❖ **When do I feel most fulfilled at work?**

This question gets to the deeper "why" behind your professional choices. Is it when you see the positive impact on customers? When you help your team grow? When you deliver a challenging project against the odds? When do you earn recognition for your expertise?

Understanding what fulfillment looks like for you ensures you're not chasing someone else's definition of success. It keeps you steady in your purpose and true to your values, even while your career changes.

Tip: Ask yourself: What professional moments would I be proud to tell a friend or mentor about?

Example: Answering the Key Questions on Passion

Imagine Daniel, a senior analyst, reflecting on these questions:

What aspects of my work energize me?

"I love designing dashboards and visual reports; it's satisfying to turn messy data into something clear and useful."

What types of challenges do I enjoy solving?

"Figuring out why performance metrics are off and telling the story behind the numbers. I get excited about connecting the dots."

When do I feel most fulfilled at work?

"When I can help leadership make better decisions with solid analysis and see my recommendations lead to real improvements."

Daniel realizes he's motivated by problem-solving, clarity, and impact. He can now seek roles that emphasize analytical storytelling, advocate for opportunities to present findings to decision-makers, and avoid positions that focus solely on routine data entry.

Understanding your motivations isn't a soft exercise; it's a strategic one. When you know what drives you, you can design a career path that maximizes engagement, reduces frustration, and ensures that the work you do is both satisfying and sustainable over the long term.

4. Articulating Your Impact and Contribution

Self-awareness is not just inward-looking. It is also the clear understanding of how you affect the world around you. Professionals who can articulate their impact are better able to communicate their value, advocate for meaningful opportunities, and align their work with what matters most. This dimension of self-awareness grounds your identity in *real-world outcomes*. It moves you beyond simply knowing your skills or motivations to recognizing the tangible results you deliver for your team, organization, or industry. Self-awareness is not only inward-looking. It means clearly understanding how you make a difference in the world around you (Drucker, 1999).

Professionals who understand their impact are more purposeful in their choices. They put their energy into high-value work. In doing so, they strengthen credibility with colleagues and leaders and learn to explain with confidence why their role matters, not just what they do. Below are three key questions to help you clarify your unique contribution:

❖ How do I make things better for others?

At its core, professional impact is about service, making someone else's work or life easier, better, or more effective.

Ask yourself:

- Do you simplify complexity for your team?
- Remove roadblocks?
- Help customers achieve their goals?
- Make communication more straightforward?

Understanding how you improve things for others helps you see the *value* you create beyond your tasks.

Tip: Ask colleagues or clients, "What do you find most helpful about working with me?"

❖ What problems do I consistently help solve?

Professionals often become go-to resources for specific challenges, even if it's not in their job description.

Reflect on the recurring themes in your work:

- Do people turn to you for conflict resolution?
- Process optimization?
- Innovative ideas?
- Customer insights?

Identifying these patterns clarifies your *brand of problem-solving* and shows where you naturally add the most value.

Tip: Review past projects or feedback to spot consistent problem-solving themes.

❖ What unique contribution do I want to be known for?

This question moves from describing your current impact to intentionally shaping your future one. It asks:

- What legacy do you want to leave?
- What do you want colleagues or industry peers to think of first when they hear your name?

By defining your desired contribution, you can make deliberate choices that build your reputation over time.

Tip: Complete this sentence: "I want to be known as the person who _____."

Example: Answering the Key Questions on Impact

Meet May, a senior operations manager reflecting on these questions:

How do I make things better for others?

"I make complex processes easier to follow, reducing stress for frontline teams."

What problems do I consistently help solve?

"Workflow inefficiencies that cause delays and frustration."

What unique contribution do I want to be known for?

"Being the person who transforms operations into smooth, reliable systems that empower teams."

May can now confidently communicate her value to senior leadership, advocate for projects aligned with her strengths, and reinforce her professional brand in performance reviews and industry conversations.

When you can clearly articulate your impact, you strengthen your credibility, guide your career decisions, and ensure that your work remains meaningful to both you and those you serve.

5. Capturing Your Learning Reflections

Self-awareness is never a single achievement. It is a practice of learning that continues through experience. Professionals who reflect deliberately on their successes and failures build adaptive capacity, deepen their insight, and avoid repeating mistakes. Self-awareness is an ongoing practice of learning from experience (Kolb, 1984). Without reflection, you risk repeating patterns that limit growth or missing opportunities to build on what works. However, with structured learning reflections, you can turn every experience into an asset. Even the difficult moments strengthen your judgment, build your skills, and shape the influence you have over time. Below are three key questions to help you capture meaningful learning:

❖ **What have been the defining moments of my career so far?**

Every professional journey includes pivotal experiences that shape who you are.

These moments might include:

- A high-profile project that stretched your skills.
- A conflict that forced you to reconsider your approach.

- A mentor's feedback that changed your mindset.

Identifying these moments helps you understand *why* you work the way you do and what truly matters to you.

Tip: List the top 3–5 moments that changed how you see your work or yourself.

❖ What did I learn from my most significant challenges?

Growth often happens in moments of difficulty.

Ask yourself:

- What didn't go as planned?
- What uncomfortable truths did you confront?
- How did you adapt?

By examining these experiences honestly, you extract lessons that make you more resilient, strategic, and prepared for the future.

Tip: Treat failures as data. What would you do differently next time?

❖ How have I changed as a professional over time?

This question connects your past to your present.

Consider:

- Which skills have you developed?
- How has your approach evolved?
- What values or goals have remained constant?

Recognizing your evolution keeps you grounded and gives you confidence in your capacity to keep growing.

Tip: Compare an early-career project to a recent one. How do your methods or mindset differ?

Example: Answering the Key Questions on Potential Growth

Meet Carlos, a marketing director reflecting on these questions:

What have been the defining moments of my career so far?

"Launching my first national campaign under a tight timeline taught me to balance creativity with discipline."

What did I learn from my biggest challenges?

"I underestimated a competitor's response once; it showed me the importance of scenario planning."

How have I changed as a professional over time?

"I've gone from reactive campaign management to building proactive, customer-centric strategies."

Carlos turns these reflections into better planning practices, shares them with his team to build collective learning, and strengthens his leadership credibility.

Documenting your reflections and looking back on them makes your growth deliberate rather than random. It transforms experience into wisdom, positioning you as a thoughtful and adaptive professional who can thrive in a changing world.

Applying the Self-Discovery Blueprint in Your Career

Your Self-Discovery Blueprint is more than a personal exercise. When used intentionally, it becomes a strategic guide for professional decision-making and communication.

With clarity about your values, strengths, motivations, and impact, you can:

- Choose opportunities that align with what truly matters to you.
- Articulate your value clearly and credibly to employers, clients, and peers.
- Build trust-based relationships through authentic communication.
- Adapt to change while staying grounded in your core identity.
- Commit to continuous learning by turning experiences into actionable insights.

Self-awareness is not a one-time exercise; it is a professional habit. By practicing it consistently, you ensure that your career choices, leadership style, and daily actions remain aligned with who you are and the impact you want to make. In this way, self-awareness becomes the essential foundation on which you can build all other aspects of professional excellence.

Section 2: Personal Brand Development

Today's professional world runs on reputation and connection, which makes personal branding essential rather than a bonus. But personal branding is often misunderstood. It's not about slick marketing, self-promotion, or putting on a fake face. It's about communicating who you really are, clearly, consistently, and authentically, so others can understand your value, trust you, and choose to work with you (Peters, 1997).

Your personal brand is the sum of the impressions you leave through your actions, your communication, and the overall experience you deliver. It's not something you can afford to go to chance. If you don't define it intentionally, others will define it for you, often in ways that don't do justice to your strengths, values, or potential (Kaputa, 2012).

That's why this section serves as a practical guide to help you develop a brand that is clear, credible, and compelling, one that aligns with who you are and where you want to go. Personal branding is not a one-time event or a checkbox to complete. It's an ongoing, strategic process of self-discovery, articulation, and consistent delivery. It requires honest self-awareness, clear and persuasive messaging, disciplined action, and a visible, reliable presence.

In this section, we'll explore three essential pillars of effective personal branding:

First, Building Your Brand Narrative. Your personal brand is not simply a list of roles you've held or a series of job titles. It's the story of who you are as a professional. A meaningful brand narrative makes your values, strengths, motivations, and aspirations clear and allows you to express them in ways that connect with colleagues, employers, clients, and collaborators. Here, you'll find practical frameworks and real examples to help you shape your story with authenticity and clarity.

Second, Designing Your Brand Action Plan. Even the most carefully defined brand is meaningless if it is not expressed consistently. In this part, you'll learn how to translate your insights into practical, sustainable habits that keep your brand active and visible. This includes setting achievable weekly goals, nurturing meaningful professional relationships, and establishing a regular routine of reflection and refinement to keep your approach sharp and effective.

Third, Building a Strong Digital Presence. In today's professional world, your online footprint is often the first, and most frequent, way people learn about you. This section will guide you on how to optimize your professional profiles, engage intentionally with your network, and contribute thoughtfully to online communities, ensuring your brand is not only visible but also credible and influential.

Building Your Brand Narrative

Your personal brand is not simply a list of roles or job titles on a résumé; it's the story of who you are as a professional (Lair et al., 2005). Crafting a meaningful narrative helps you clarify your values, strengths, motivations, and aspirations, and communicate them in a way that resonates with employers, colleagues, clients, and collaborators.

A strong narrative does more than help you stand out in a competitive market. It helps people *understand you*. Prospective employers or partners aren't just evaluating your qualifications, they're asking: Who is this person? What do they stand for? What difference will they make? (Labrecque et al., 2011)

Building your brand narrative isn't about exaggeration or spin. At its core, it's the intentional, structured story you tell about what you believe, what you bring to the table, and what you're committed to delivering (Shepherd, 2005). When your narrative is well-developed, the way you see yourself matches the way others see you. This creates a clear and authentic identity that people can rely on and recall.

A thoughtfully crafted brand narrative offers several essential benefits:

- **Clarity:**
  Building your narrative requires reflection. It asks you to define the strengths, values, and experiences that are uniquely yours. It helps you see patterns in your career journey that reveal what you do best and why it matters. This clarity empowers you to speak confidently about your skills and differentiators in any setting, from interviews to performance reviews to informal networking conversations. It also gives you the language to position yourself clearly in a crowded, competitive marketplace.

- **Focus:**
  Beyond knowing your strengths, your narrative helps you identify what truly aligns with your deeper purpose and goals. By clarifying your "why," you can make more intentional choices about the roles you pursue, the environments in which you thrive, and the projects you prioritize. Your narrative acts as a strategic filter, helping you avoid opportunities that don't fit your long-term vision and lean into those that do, ensuring your career development remains deliberate and aligned.

- **Connection:**
  Stories are inherently human. They resonate, engage, and build trust in a way that lists of skills or credentials alone cannot. A well-crafted narrative invites others to connect with you on both a personal and professional level. It provides a bridge for colleagues, employers, clients, and collaborators to understand not just what you do, but why you do it, and why they should trust and engage with you. In this way, your story becomes an invaluable tool for building authentic, lasting professional relationships.

A well-framed narrative also ensures consistency across all your professional communication. It becomes the common thread that ties together everything you share about yourself:

- Your résumé summarizes your achievements through the lens of your story.
- Your LinkedIn profile, which offers a public, accessible version of your professional journey and promise.
- Your interview responses bring your experiences to life in a relatable, impactful way.
- Your informal networking conversations become opportunities to communicate your purpose clearly and memorably.

By anchoring all of these touchpoints in a cohesive, authentic narrative, you reduce confusion, strengthen credibility, and ensure your audience receives a clear, compelling, and trustworthy message about who you are and what you stand for.

In short, your brand narrative is not simply a story you tell others; it is the foundation of how you navigate your career, communicate your value, and build meaningful, lasting connections in your professional world.

Storytelling humanizes your brand, sparks emotional engagement, and reveals the depth behind your achievements. Figure 3: the 5-Part Brand Story Wheel gives you a personal yet professional structure to turn scattered experiences into a strategic narrative arc that shows not only what you've done but who you've become.

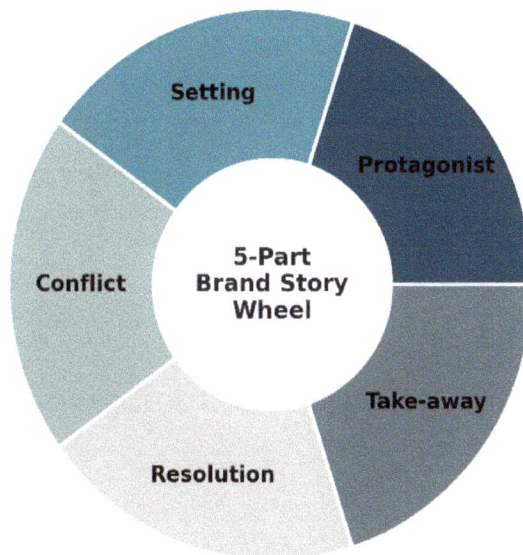

Figure 3: The 5-Part Brand Story Wheel

Element	Description
Protagonist	Who are you? Describe your personality, values, worldview, and guiding principles.
Setting	Where have you come from? Share relevant life contexts, industries, cultures, or environments that have shaped you.
Conflict	What challenges or turning points have shaped your journey? Include personal or professional adversity, transitions, or decisions that tested you.
Resolution	How did you respond to those moments? Explain the actions you took, what you changed or overcame, and what strengths emerged.
Takeaway	What insight, value, or mission now defines you? Articulate the message you want others to remember, your professional "why."

Professional Tips for Developing Your Narrative

- **Start with real moments**: Don't fabricate drama. Look for the meaningful moments in your actual journey, career changes, turning points, failures, mentors, feedback, or breakthroughs.
- **Balance vulnerability with strength**: It's okay to mention challenges, as long as you show growth and resolution. Adversity is powerful when paired with insight.
- **Make it relevant**: Always tie the story back to the present. Your audience should understand how your past has equipped you to add value today.
- **Keep it adaptable**: While your core story remains the same, you can emphasize different aspects depending on the context. For a job interview, you may highlight achievements; in a panel discussion, you may emphasize values.

Applying the Framework

Let's look at how this works in practice. Suppose you're an engineer in the Oil and Gas industry. Your story might sound like this:

- **Protagonist**: This is who you are at your core, your professional character. For the engineer, it's about valuing safety, integrity, and innovative problem-solving. You're not just an employee turning a profit. You see energy production as a responsibility to people and the environment. That establishes you as someone with strong ethics, vision, and a commitment to doing the right thing, even when it's hard.
- **Setting**: This is the context that shaped you. You began your career on offshore rigs and in demanding field environments. You learned under extreme conditions that required precision, resilience, and decisive action.

- **Conflict**: This part reveals the challenges and turning points in your career. You faced operational failures, safety incidents, and environmental risks that forced you to question the industry's standard practices.
- **Resolution**: This describes how you responded to those challenges. You didn't ignore the issues. You sought advanced certifications, joined cross-functional teams, and led an initiative that reduced downtime and safety incidents by 40%.
- **Takeaway**: This is the key message you want others to remember about you. For this engineer, it's the belief that safe, efficient, and sustainable energy production is possible through technical excellence, collaborative leadership, and continuous improvement.

When you apply the 5-Part Brand Story Framework, you transform your professional experience from a list of roles into a compelling, authentic narrative that truly resonates. By naming who you are, what shaped you, the trials you met, and the values that guide you, you offer others a professional identity that is both clear and trustworthy. By applying this structure, you move beyond listing jobs or skills and create a narrative that humanizes your brand and resonates with your audience.

Example of Oil and Gas Engineer Brand Narrative

"I launched my career as a field engineer working on offshore platforms and remote drilling sites, environments that demanded absolute precision, resilience under pressure, and an unwavering commitment to safety. Those formative years shaped my understanding that the Oil and Gas industry is not merely about extracting resources, but about protecting people, preserving the environment, and maintaining the integrity of complex operations. Confronting the costs of downtime, seeing safety incidents with lasting human consequences, and becoming aware of environmental risks pushed me to question the way our industry operates. These challenges weren't just technical puzzles; they were ethical imperatives that compelled me to question the status quo and seek more effective solutions.

Driven by that responsibility, I pursued advanced engineering certifications and immersed myself in cross-functional teams focused on elevating safety standards and streamlining operational processes. One of my most significant achievements was leading the redesign of our maintenance and inspection protocols, which resulted in a 40% reduction in unplanned downtime and safety incidents. This initiative didn't just improve productivity; it enhanced workforce well-being and demonstrated what's possible when rigorous technical standards meet genuine care for people.

Today, I approach engineering as both a technical craft and a moral duty. I'm committed to fostering collaboration across disciplines, promoting continuous improvement, and ensuring every project delivers safe, efficient, and sustainable energy solutions. For me, engineering is more than a career; it is a promise to provide reliable energy in a way that respects people, communities, and the planet we all share."

Your brand story goes beyond being a narrative. It serves as a strategic asset, shaping perception, self-understanding, and the way you pursue opportunities. When you articulate your story with intention, you don't just stand out, you stand for something. And that, ultimately, is what defines a compelling personal brand.

Brand Action Plan Template

Even the most thoughtfully defined brand is meaningless if it isn't expressed consistently (Rampersad, 2008). That's why your personal brand must move from abstract idea to concrete, repeatable action. A Brand Action Plan helps you translate your insights into daily and weekly habits that reinforce your promise and keep your brand visible.

This includes setting small, achievable goals, such as writing one insightful LinkedIn post per week or meeting with a new industry contact each month. Consistent action, over time, compounds to strengthen your credibility and visibility (Harris & Rae, 2011).

It also involves regular reflection and adjustment. Professionals who treat personal branding as an ongoing practice, not a one-time marketing exercise, maintain relevance, trust, and alignment with evolving goals and contexts (Montoya & Vandehey, 2002).

The Brand Action Plan Template consists of three key components: Weekly Branding Goals, Networking Intentions, and Monthly Reflection, each supporting sustained, visible, and strategic personal branding. (See Figure 4).

Brand Action Plan Template

✓ **Weekly Branding Goals**
Define specific, achievable actions that reinforce your brand each wek

✓ **Networking Intentions**
Deliberately cultivating meaningful professional relationships

✓ **Monthly Reflection**
Regular assessment and adjustment

Figure 4: Brand Action Plan Template

Below are the three core components of the template, explained in detail:

- **Weekly Branding Goals:**
This section encourages you to define specific, achievable actions that reinforce your brand each week. Examples include writing one thoughtful LinkedIn post that demonstrates your expertise, commenting meaningfully on two industry peers' posts to build visibility and credibility, or sharing a relevant article with personal insight. These activities ensure that your brand remains active and visible in professional networks. Weekly goals should be realistic and tailored to your industry, audience, and communication style. Over time, these small, regular actions compound to strengthen your reputation and expand your reach.

- **Networking Intentions:**
Building a strong personal brand also depends on cultivating meaningful professional relationships. The networking intentions section prompts you to be deliberate about growing and maintaining your connections. For instance, you might set a goal to reach out to one new contact each week, follow up with people you met at a recent conference, or schedule a virtual coffee with a mentor or colleague. These intentional networking activities help you stay top of mind, uncover new opportunities, and reinforce your brand promise in one-on-one settings. They also ensure that your network remains diverse, engaged, and relevant to your professional goals.

- **Monthly Reflection:**
Sustainable personal branding requires regular assessment and adjustment. The monthly reflection component encourages you to pause and evaluate your efforts. Ask yourself: *What is resonating with my audience? What feedback or engagement have I received? What activities felt authentic and impactful? What needs adjusting or improving?* This reflection ensures your strategy remains adaptive and relevant. It helps you identify emerging opportunities, refine your messaging, and address any disconnect between your intended brand and how it is perceived. Over time, this disciplined reflection builds self-awareness and strengthens the authenticity and effectiveness of your brand.

When used consistently, the Brand Action Plan Template transforms personal branding from an abstract goal into a repeatable, sustainable practice. It guarantees that your brand is defined with clarity, expressed consistently, strengthened with strategy, and adapted as it grows. By committing to regular action, intentional networking, and honest reflection, you build a professional identity that is both authentic and influential, positioning you for credibility, opportunity, and long-term success.

Example: Lina develops a 4-week branding sprint.

- **Weekly Goals:**
  - Week 1: Publish a story about her experience with staff-led scheduling improvements.
  - Week 2: Comment meaningfully on two industry leader posts.
  - Week 3: Share a book excerpt on empathetic leadership with a personal takeaway.
  - Week 4: Reshare a colleague's article with an added insight.
- **Networking Intentions:**
  - Schedule one virtual coffee each week with someone in her field.
  - Follow up with conference attendees she met last month.

- **Monthly Reflection:**
  - What resonated? Her story post received 200% more engagement.
  - What needs adjusting? Her tone in comments felt too formal, so she decided to adopt a more conversational approach.

Outcome:

With the template, Lina moves from passive content consumption to strategic brand building, aligned, visible, and intentional.

Building a Strong Digital Presence

In today's professional world, your online presence is often the first and most frequent way people learn about you (Labrecque et al., 2011). Unlike a static résumé, your digital footprint is a dynamic, evolving representation of your expertise, values, and professional promise.

Establishing a compelling online identity is foundational for effective digital networking. A profile alone does little. Its value comes alive when you give it attention and use it as a space for real connection and contribution. A strong digital presence demonstrates that you are not only knowledgeable in your field but also accessible, engaged, and committed to continuous learning and collaboration.

A strong digital presence is built on three essentials: Professional Profile Optimization, Consistent, Intentional Engagement, and Joining Digital Communities (See Figure 5).

Building a Strong Digital Presence

Professional Profile Optimization
Step 1
Enhancing online profiles with a clear value proposition, professional photo, and notable achievements

Consistent, Intentional Engagement
Step 2
Commenting on posts, sharing resources, and interacting in a meaningful way

Join Digital Communities
Step 3
Participating in professional groups, forums, and networks

Participating in professional groups, forums, and networks

Figure 5: The three essential steps for building a strong and sustainable digital presence

Below are three key steps to help you build and maintain a professional digital presence that reinforces your personal brand and opens doors to new opportunities:

Step 1: Professional Profile Optimization

Profile Optimization: Ensuring your online profiles, particularly LinkedIn, clearly articulate your value proposition with a professional photo, compelling summary, and concrete achievements. To ensure it accurately and powerfully represents you:

- Use a high-resolution, professional headshot that is friendly, approachable, and appropriate for your industry.
- Craft a headline that goes beyond your job title to highlight your expertise, unique value, and impact. For example, instead of "Marketing Manager," consider "Marketing Strategist Driving Customer-Centric Growth."
- Write a compelling summary that tells your professional story, articulates your values and goals, and communicates your value proposition.
- Highlight achievements with measurable outcomes, not just responsibilities. This demonstrates real impact and credibility.
- Include volunteer roles, certifications, and endorsements to showcase your commitment to growth, community, and well-rounded expertise.

Step 2: Consistent, Intentional Engagement

A polished profile is only the starting point. Building a strong digital presence also requires ongoing, authentic interaction. Intentional engagement demonstrates that you are actively involved in your field, willing to share insights, and supportive of your peers. Consider these practices:

- Comment on relevant posts with thoughtful, original insights that add value to the conversation.
- Share helpful resources and industry news that reflect your expertise and keep your network informed.
- Ask informed questions in online forums or group discussions to demonstrate curiosity and invite meaningful dialogue.
- Congratulate others on milestones and achievements, reinforcing your reputation as a supportive, engaged professional.

Step 3: Join Digital Communities

Building a strong digital presence also means finding and contributing to professional communities where you can exchange ideas, learn, and build relationships:

- Participate in LinkedIn groups, Slack workspaces, and other interest-based networks aligned with your field or goals.

- Attend virtual conferences, webinars, and industry meetups to expand your professional network and stay current with the latest trends and best practices.
- Be visible and contribute value without immediate expectations, showing you're there to share, learn, and support, not just to self-promote.

A strong digital presence is not built overnight. It requires consistent effort, strategic clarity, and authentic connection. By optimizing your profile, engaging meaningfully, and actively participating in digital communities, you ensure that your online identity is not just professional but genuinely compelling. In doing so, you position yourself as a visible, trusted, and valuable member of your professional ecosystem, ready to connect, collaborate, and lead in the digital age. This is not about relentless self-promotion. It's about being visible, helpful, and authentic in ways that build credibility and invite collaboration.

Case Study: Lama's Strategic Digital Transformation

Background:

Lama is a mid-level communications officer at a regional nonprofit organization focused on health education. Despite having over a decade of field experience, she felt overlooked for leadership opportunities and often received limited external visibility. A colleague once told her, "You're doing great work, but nobody outside this team knows it."

Motivated to shift this narrative, Lama embarked on a six-month journey to build a more substantial digital presence, guided by three pillars: profile optimization, intentional engagement, and active community participation.

Step 1: Professional Profile Optimization

Lama began with a full review of her LinkedIn profile, treating it not as a digital résumé but as a living representation of her professional identity.

- She updated her headshot to a high-resolution, friendly, and professionally styled photograph.
- She restructured her headline to reflect her value, not just her title:

"Strategic Communications | Health Equity Advocate | Amplifying Stories that Inspire Policy and Change"

- Her new summary blended her technical background with her mission:

"With over 10 years of experience in public health communication, I help translate complex health information into messages that inform and empower. Passionate about health literacy, I build campaigns that foster behavior change, stakeholder trust, and long-term impact."

- She reframed her experience section to include measurable outcomes (e.g., "Increased community event turnout by 45% through multi-channel messaging").

- She added certifications in digital strategy and public speaking, listed her volunteer role with a local women's health initiative, and requested endorsements from former collaborators.

This complete overhaul transformed her profile into a compelling story, not just of what she did, but why it mattered and where she was headed.

Step 2: Consistent, Intentional Engagement

Rather than sporadically scrolling through social feeds, Lama developed a weekly engagement habit:

- On Mondays, she commented on industry articles shared by thought leaders in health communication, offering short insights or posing questions.
- On Wednesdays, she shared resources, like toolkits and webinars, tailored to nonprofit professionals in her network.
- On Fridays, she congratulated peers on promotions, speaking engagements, and published work, offering personalized encouragement.

One post, a short commentary on a newly published report about digital misinformation, sparked an unexpected conversation with a senior policy advisor. This single interaction led to an invitation to participate in a virtual panel discussion titled "Health Messaging in the Digital Age."

"I realized that engagement isn't about being seen. It's about showing up—consistently, helpfully, and with a point of view." – Lama

Step 3: Joining Digital Communities

To broaden her exposure and deepen her professional dialogue, Lama joined three targeted digital groups:

1. A LinkedIn group for public health communicators, where she contributed to discussions on campaign ethics and cultural sensitivity.
2. A Slack workspace for nonprofit digital strategists, where she discovered tools to improve campaign analytics.
3. An email-based community for women in social impact leadership, which featured monthly virtual mixers.

She also began attending webinars hosted by international NGOs and posed thoughtful questions during Q&A sessions, earning direct messages from panelists and attendees who valued her perspective.

One of these connections, a director at a regional WHO office, later introduced her to a consultancy project that aligned perfectly with her expertise.

Results After Six Months

Lama's digital efforts produced tangible and intangible benefits:

- **Visibility:** Her LinkedIn profile views increased by 300%, and she was added to two speaking rosters without applying.
- **Opportunities:** She was invited to mentor two early-career professionals and was shortlisted for a fellowship she hadn't known existed until a LinkedIn contact forwarded it.
- **Confidence:** Most importantly, Lama began to see herself not just as a doer, but as a visible contributor in her field.

Digital presence is not self-promotion. It's self-definition. You're shaping the narrative of your professional value every day, one action at a time.

Building your personal brand is more than defining your values, message, and audience; it's about translating insight into intentional action. The frameworks and examples in this section show that effective branding is both structured and personal. By clarifying your promise and purpose, you give yourself and others a clear and compelling way to understand what you stand for.

These implementation examples bring tools to life. When applied consistently and with reflection, they help professionals not only define their brand but also embody and evolve it over time. But defining your brand is only the beginning. The real challenge lies in living it consistently.

Section 3: Maintaining Consistency and Engagement

Building a personal brand isn't just about writing the perfect bio or declaring your values once. It's a long-term commitment to living your message consistently and engaging meaningfully with the world around you (Montoya & Vandehey, 2002). In professional life, trust is earned through steady, reliable action. A credible personal brand emerges from the disciplined habit of showing up the same way across every interaction, while remaining flexible enough to grow and evolve over time (Rampersad, 2008).

Consistency is the bedrock of trust. Clients, colleagues, and your professional network need to know they can rely on you, whether they're reading your LinkedIn profile, attending a presentation, or working with you on a project (Harris & Rae, 2011). Consistency means showing up with the same values and tone so your professional promise can be trusted in any setting. This creates a stable, recognizable identity that people can understand, remember, and choose to work with. Importantly, consistency doesn't mean being rigid or robotic. It's about adapting to different contexts while ensuring your core remains unmistakably clear and true (Kaputa, 2012).

But consistency on its own isn't enough. A brand that is perfectly consistent but lifeless will quickly become irrelevant. Engagement is what brings your brand to life. It's how you show that you're not just present, but actively participating, listening, responding, contributing, and helping your field move forward. Engagement is the difference between simply broadcasting your message and actually having a conversation. Professionals who commit to authentic engagement don't just become recognizable; they become relevant, respected, and valued members of their professional communities.

Meaningful engagement signals that you care not only about your own reputation but also about the success and growth of others. Sharing insights, acknowledging other people's contributions, asking thoughtful questions, and supporting collective learning all help build trust, loyalty, and goodwill. Engagement transforms your brand from a static promise into a dynamic relationship with your audience, one built on mutual respect and genuine contribution.

The professional world today moves quickly and stays tightly connected, which makes balancing consistency and engagement essential. This section will help you understand how to align your visual, verbal, and behavioral signals so that your brand remains cohesive and trustworthy across all platforms and interactions. You'll also learn how to keep your brand dynamic and engaging through intentional, ongoing participation that demonstrates your commitment to your field, your values, and the people you serve.

Finally, this section doesn't just explain why these principles matter; it offers practical, proven tools to help you maintain them over time. From weekly engagement trackers to strategic content calendars, to the Three-to-One Rule for balanced interaction, you'll gain frameworks to make consistency and engagement sustainable and effective habits. Together, these practices will help you develop a personal brand that is not just clear and credible but also compelling, adaptive, and genuinely influential in your professional world.

Building Trust Through Consistency and Authentic Engagement

Trust is the currency of professional relationships, built on the foundation of consistency and authentic engagement. Whether people meet you online or in person, they should experience the same credible and authentic version of you. Consistency doesn't mean being rigid or formulaic; it means that your values, message, and tone remain clear, intentional, and reliable. Without this disciplined consistency, even the best-crafted brand can appear fragmented, confusing, or untrustworthy.

Consistency has three critical dimensions that work together to strengthen your professional credibility:

- **Visual Consistency:**
  Visual cues are often the first signals people receive about your professional brand. A consistent visual identity builds recognition and projects professionalism. This means using unified design elements, such as color palettes, fonts, and images, across all your platforms (Van Dijck, 2013). Whether it's your LinkedIn profile, personal website, or presentation slides, the look and feel should reinforce the same message.

- **Verbal Consistency:**
  Your words carry your brand's promise. Verbal consistency ensures that whether someone reads your bio, listens to your presentation, or exchanges emails with you, they hear the same core message and values (Shepherd, 2005). It means maintaining a clear, focused tone that matches your brand personality, whether formal, approachable, technical, or inspiring.

- **Behavioral Consistency:**
  Ultimately, your brand is defined by what you do, not just what you say or show. Behavioral consistency is about aligning your actions with your brand promise (Lair et al., 2005). It means demonstrating reliability, ethical conduct, and collaborative behavior in every setting, from meetings and emails to interviews and networking events.

But consistency alone isn't enough. A brand that is perfectly consistent but lifeless will quickly become irrelevant. Engagement is what brings your brand to life. It shows you're not just present, but participating, listening, responding, contributing, and helping your field move forward (Labrecque et al., 2011).

Meaningful engagement demonstrates you care not only about your own reputation but about the success and growth of others. Sharing insights, acknowledging contributions, asking thoughtful questions, and supporting collective learning all contribute to building trust, loyalty, and goodwill (Peters, 1997). Engagement transforms your brand from a static promise into a dynamic relationship with your audience, one built on mutual respect and genuine contribution.

Examples of authentic engagement include:

- Sharing professional insights, lessons learned, and reflections that help others grow.
- Asking thoughtful questions and acknowledging others' contributions fosters shared learning.
- Actively participating in industry events, online forums, or professional groups to stay visible and connected.
- Building thought leadership through content that sparks meaningful discussion and offers practical solutions.

- By pairing consistency with authentic engagement, you create a brand that others recognize with clarity and trust, one that remains vibrant and adaptable over time. When you commit to these practices, you establish yourself as a professional who is both reliable and relevant, a trusted partner, advisor, and leader in your field.

Sustaining Engagement: Tools for Long-Term Brand Presence

Engagement isn't about broadcasting your message repeatedly. It's about building genuine connections. Professionals who commit to authentic engagement become not only recognizable but also respected and valued members of their professional communities (Harris & Rae, 2011). To maintain momentum and continue growing your presence, the following tools can help you stay consistent, intentional, and connected to your audience:

1. Weekly Engagement Tracker

Purpose: Helps you measure and reflect on how frequently and meaningfully you engage with your professional network.

How It Works: Create a simple chart or digital tracker with categories such as:

- Posts shared
- Comments made
- Messages sent
- New connections added
- Events attended (webinars, panels, discussions)

Example:

At the end of the week, Sarah, a leadership consultant, logs the following:

- Shared one original post reflecting on a recent coaching session
- Commented on three peers' articles
- Reached out to two new connections from a virtual conference
- Participated in a LinkedIn Live session and contributed a question in the chat

This weekly reflection helps Sarah ensure she's showing up regularly and not relying solely on self-promotion. Over time, the tracker reveals trends in engagement and areas where she may want to diversify or deepen her presence.

2. Content Calendar

Purpose: Keeps your brand presence proactive rather than reactive by helping you plan what to say, when, and why.

How It Works: Map out a month (or quarter) of planned content aligned with your brand themes. Your calendar might include:

- Thought leadership posts (e.g., lessons from your work)
- Industry insights or curated resources
- Behind-the-scenes moments (e.g., how you prepare for a keynote)
- Personal reflections that connect to your professional identity

Example:

David, a healthcare HR director, creates a monthly plan:

- **Week 1:** Share a takeaway from a leadership summit
- **Week 2:** Comment on an article about employee wellbeing
- **Week 3:** Post a quote from a mentor and how it shaped their leadership style
- **Week 4:** Reshare a colleague's post on inclusive hiring, adding their own perspective

Value: By planning content, David avoids last-minute scrambling and maintains a consistent rhythm that reinforces his brand narrative.

3. The "Three-to-One Rule"

Purpose: Keeps your engagement balanced and audience-focused by encouraging generosity and interaction over self-promotion.

How It Works: The "Three-to-One Rule" works by ensuring your online interactions are weighted toward generosity and community building rather than self-promotion (See Figure 6).

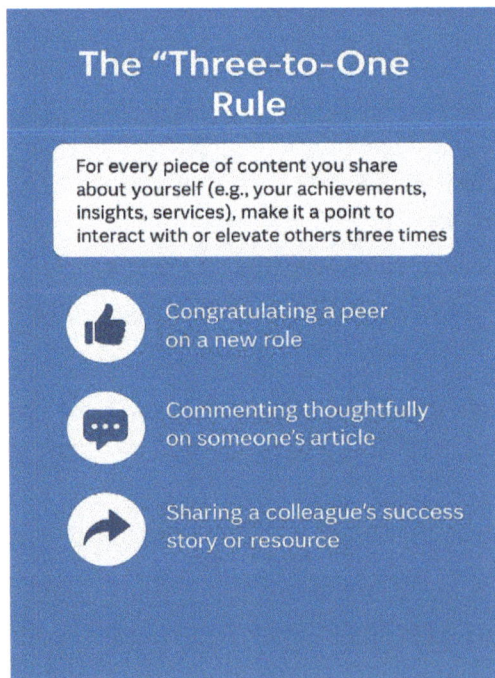

The "Three-to-One Rule

For every piece of content you share about yourself (e.g., your achievements, insights, services), make it a point to interact with or elevate others three times

👍 Congratulating a peer on a new role

💬 Commenting thoughtfully on someone's article

➡️ Sharing a colleague's success story or resource

Figure 6: The "Three-to-One Rule"

Example:

Alaa, a communications strategist, posts about her new article in a trade magazine. That same week, she:

1. Comments on a junior colleague's post about graduating from a professional program
2. Reshares her mentor's recent webinar with a note about its value
3. Sends a direct message to a former teammate to celebrate their promotion

Alaa's actions foster goodwill and trust, positioning her as someone who contributes to the community, not just her visibility.

These tools are not just about metrics; they're about cultivating relationships, reinforcing credibility, and sustaining momentum. Used consistently, they ensure your personal brand isn't just seen, it's felt, remembered, and trusted. By committing to these practices, you build a personal brand that is clear, credible, and compelling.

Finally, treat consistency and engagement not as burdens, but as practices of presence. Your brand isn't static; it's a relationship with your audience. Like all relationships, it requires intentional effort, alignment, and care.

Executive Snapshot – Chapter 1: Authentic Presence

Authentic Presence is where professional credibility begins. Throughout this chapter, you clarified core values, surfaced the narrative that links your past to your future, and learned to embody those values through consistent micro-behaviors. Remember: people trust what they can predict. The more explicitly your actions echo your stated principles, the faster others grant you authority. Use the recap below to cement the habits that translate intention into observable integrity.

✓ Clarify your core values and align daily choices with them.
✓ Craft a genuine personal brand rooted in credibility, not self-promotion.
✓ Tell a concise brand narrative that links past experience to future impact.
✓ Model organizational values to act as a cultural ambassador.
✓ Practice self-awareness rituals (journaling, 360° feedback) to stay congruent.
✓ Demonstrate consistency: small, repeated actions build trust faster than words.

Reflection Question: Which daily habit will you adjust this week to mirror your stated values better?

Chapter Two: Communication Mastery

Communication is one of the most powerful tools you have as a professional. By fostering trust and shaping perceptions, it transforms your ideas into actionable results. Yet too often, people mistake communication for simply talking or sending messages. True mastery of communication is something much more profound. It's the ability to share your ideas clearly, genuinely understand others, and create shared meaning that drives collaboration and progress.

At its heart, speaking your truth isn't about dominating conversations or constantly proving you're right. It's about expressing your thoughts, values, and intentions in a way that is authentic, respectful, and effective. It takes courage to be clear about what you stand for, humility to truly listen and adapt, and awareness to make sure your words, actions, and presence are aligned.

In today's fast-paced, interconnected workplace, the stakes for communication have never been higher. Teams often work across departments, time zones, and even cultures. Complex challenges demand precise coordination and mutual understanding. Minor misunderstandings can quickly escalate into costly mistakes, missed opportunities, or damaged relationships. On the other hand, clear, transparent, and empathetic communication accelerates alignment, reduces friction, and builds the trust and confidence that make great work possible.

Mastering communication means developing both internal and external skills. It requires self-awareness of your intentions, emotional intelligence to read the room, and practical techniques to deliver your message effectively.

This chapter will help you strengthen your communication mastery through three essential, interconnected principles. Clarity is about delivering your ideas as intended, using clear language and preparation to prevent misunderstandings and build trust. Empathy and Active Listening transform your conversations from surface-level exchanges into genuine dialogue by encouraging you to understand other people's perspectives and respond thoughtfully and truly. Non-Verbal Intelligence ensures that your body language, facial expressions, and tone of voice support and reinforce your message, helping you come across as authentic and credible.

These principles aren't optional extras; they're core competencies for anyone who wants to communicate effectively, have a meaningful impact, and build lasting professional relationships. As you work through this chapter, you'll find practical tools, proven frameworks, and real-world examples to help you apply these skills, elevate your professional presence, and empower you to speak your truth with confidence, empathy, and integrity.

Section 1: The Power of Clarity in Communication

Clarity is not a luxury or a bonus in any professional environment. It is an essential skill that transforms communication from a simple exchange of words into impactful, effective action (Heath & Heath, 2007). In fast-paced, complex, and highly collaborative settings, clear communication often marks the difference between smooth execution and costly confusion. It ensures that your ideas are not just shared but truly understood as you intend, reducing errors, misalignment, and wasted effort while fostering trust and efficiency within your team (Clampitt, 2016).

Clarity is what cuts through the noise. It brings order to chaos by turning ideas into action, instructions into results, and vision into collective purpose (Heath & Heath, 2007). Clear communicators enable their teams to work smarter by making goals, expectations, and next steps unmistakably clear. They help reduce errors and rework, break down silos, and build trust by showing respect for their colleagues' time and intelligence. At its core, clarity is a leadership practice because when you communicate clearly, you empower others to succeed (Adler et al., 2019).

This section will guide you step by step through the principles and techniques you need to become a more intentional, effective, and respected communicator. Ultimately, clarity is not just about conveying your own ideas; it's about leading others (Gallo, 2014).

Beyond structuring your message, you'll discover the power of choosing the right language: using straightforward, jargon-free words that respect and include your audience, regardless of their background or expertise (Plain Language Action and Information Network, 2011). You'll learn how to pause before responding, giving yourself the space to organize your thoughts clearly, even under pressure. You'll replace rambling or confusing answers with confident, well-framed explanations (Clampitt, 2016).

This section also covers the essential role of non-verbal communication. Your tone of voice, facial expressions, gestures, and posture all need to work together with your words to deliver a consistent and credible message. When these elements align, they reinforce your message and project authenticity and confidence.

By mastering these techniques, you'll not only become a more effective communicator yourself, but you'll also help elevate your entire team's performance. Clarity drives productive collaboration, minimizes conflict, accelerates decision-making, and fosters trust at every level of an organization.

Ultimately, clarity in communication is a defining element of leadership. It's about ensuring that every email, meeting, presentation, or conversation leads to shared understanding, alignment, and confident action. It's the professional discipline of turning complex or sensitive ideas into accessible, persuasive, and motivating messages (Heath & Heath, 2007). Clear communication sharpens your credibility and influence, helping create a culture that values transparency and drives tangible results.

Communicating with Purpose: Mastering the PREP Framework for Clarity

Achieving clarity is not about oversimplifying complex ideas; it's about presenting them in a structured, purposeful, and accessible way (Clampitt, 2016). This requires you to think carefully about what you want to say, why it matters, and how to deliver it most effectively. One proven approach to achieve this is the PREP Framework, a simple yet powerful communication template designed to help you organize your thoughts logically and persuasively.

One effective way to achieve structured, persuasive communication is by using the PREP Framework, Point, Reason, Example, Point (Restated), which ensures your message flows logically and resonates with your audience (see Figure 7).

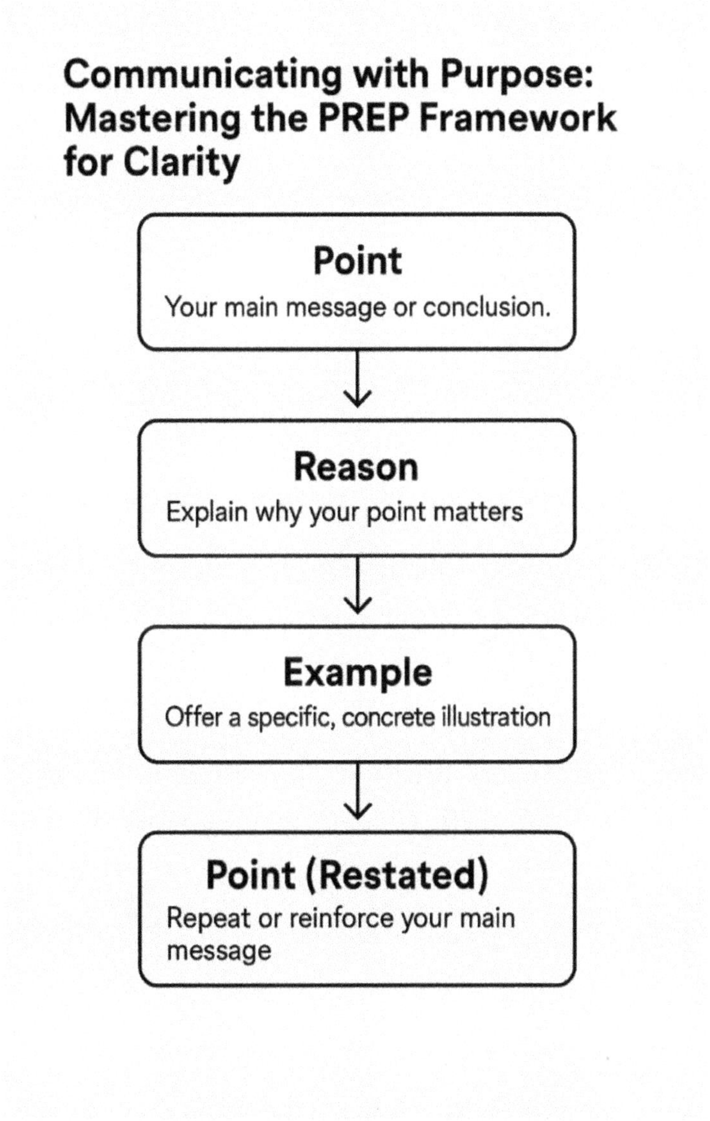

Communicating with Purpose: Mastering the PREP Framework for Clarity

Point
Your main message or conclusion.

↓

Reason
Explain why your point matters

↓

Example
Offer a specific, concrete illustration

↓

Point (Restated)
Repeat or reinforce your main message

Figure 7: The PREP Framework

The **PREP Framework** stands for:

- **Point:**
  Your main message or conclusion. State this clearly and directly. This is what you want your audience to remember above all else. Avoid hedging or vague language here.

- **Reason:**
  Explain why your point matters. Provide justification or context to make your argument compelling. This step connects your idea to your audience's interests or needs, helping them see its relevance.

- **Example:**
  Offer a specific, concrete illustration that supports your point. Examples make abstract ideas tangible, relatable, and memorable. They also demonstrate that your point is grounded in reality, not just theory.

- **Point (Restated):**
  Repeat or reinforce your main message to ensure it sticks. This final step helps anchor your conclusion in your listener's mind, leaving them with a clear understanding of what you want them to take away.

Example: Using the PREP Framework

Scenario: A team lead needs to address the importance of adopting a new project management tool during a team meeting.

Point:

I strongly recommend that we adopt the new project management software for all upcoming projects.

Reason:

It will enhance our ability to track progress, manage resources, and communicate transparently, which is crucial given the increasing complexity of our projects.

Example:

For instance, during the last project, we struggled with version control and missed a critical update because our communication was fragmented. The new tool integrates messaging, scheduling, and file sharing in one place, reducing the risk of such oversights.

Point (Restated):

By adopting this new software, we'll streamline our workflows and enhance our team's efficiency and accountability.

The power of PREP lies in its simplicity and adaptability. It gives your communication a logical flow that guides your audience step by step. Instead of overwhelming them with unstructured information or rambling arguments, you deliver your message with precision and persuasive force. The PREP Framework works in a range of situations, from meetings and presentations to difficult conversations and emails, wherever clarity is required.

Practical Strategies for Clarity

Communicating with clarity is not an innate talent reserved for a lucky few; it is a skill that can be learned, practiced, and mastered. It requires intentionality, discipline, and awareness of your audience's needs. Professionals who communicate with clarity don't just convey information; they guide understanding, inspire confidence, and drive action. This section explores practical strategies you can adopt to become a clearer, more compelling communicator.

1. Take a Moment to Pause and Collect Your Thoughts

One of the simplest strategies for clarity is pausing before responding. In high-pressure or fast-paced environments, people often feel compelled to answer immediately, leading to rambling explanations or unclear instructions. By pausing, even briefly, you create space to organize your thoughts and consider your listener's perspective (Heath & Heath, 2007).

Example:

Imagine a senior engineer asked on the spot about why a design change is necessary. Without pausing, they might launch into a technical monologue full of jargon. But by taking a moment, they can frame their response accessibly:

"That's a great question. In simple terms, this change improves safety by reducing pressure fluctuations that can lead to leaks."

Pausing signals confidence and respect. It tells your audience you care enough to consider your words carefully. Leaders who master this habit often inspire calm and credibility in their teams.

2. Use Straightforward Language – Avoid Jargon or Overcomplication

Clarity thrives on simplicity. Avoid jargon or overcomplicated phrasing. By choosing plain words, you respect your audience's time and intelligence (Plain Language Action and Information Network, 2011).

Example:

A financial analyst presenting to the board says: "Our EBITDA margin shows a higher profit because fixed costs stayed level while revenue increased."

A clearer version might be: "Our operating profit margin improved because our fixed costs stayed the same while revenue increased."

By choosing plain, accessible words, you respect your audience's time and intelligence. You also demonstrate mastery of your subject. Anyone can hide behind jargon, but true experts can explain complex ideas.

Tip: Before sending an important email or attending a meeting, review your message. Ask: *Would someone outside my field understand this?* If not, simplify.

3. Maintain a Structured Approach in Both Written and Spoken Communication

Structure is what turns scattered thoughts into clear, compelling messages. It guides your audience through your reasoning step by step, making your points more straightforward to follow and remember. Even the best ideas can feel confusing or get lost if they're delivered without an intentional framework (Clampitt, 2016). While you've already seen how the PREP Framework can help clarify your message, it's essential to recognize that many other structures are equally valuable depending on your context and purpose. For example:

- **Problem–Solution–Benefit**: Ideal for proposals or persuasive pitches, this approach defines the challenge, presents your recommended solution, and explains the advantages it delivers.
- **What? So What? Now What?** This structure helps explain analyses or decisions, laying out the facts or situation (What?), describing their importance or implications (So What?), and identifying next steps or actions (*Now What?*).
- **Past–Present–Future**: This approach is ideal for storytelling, updates, or vision-setting, as it reviews past events, assesses the current state, and outlines plans or goals for the future.

When you choose the appropriate structure based on your audience and purpose, you make sure your message resonates and inspires action. Structured communication signals professionalism, preparation, and respect for your listener's time and attention.

Example:

To illustrate how these three structures can help you deliver the same core message in different, practical ways, let's look at a single scenario from multiple angles. Imagine you're a project manager tasked with updating senior leadership about challenges in your digital transformation project. Your goal is to clearly articulate the issue, propose a solution, and secure their support for the next steps. Below are three structured ways to communicate this message, each tailored to a different framework.

Problem–Solution–Benefit:

- **Problem:** "We're experiencing delays in our digital transformation project because some teams are struggling to adopt the new system."
- **Solution:** "We plan to deliver targeted training and hands-on support to help these teams adapt more confidently."
- **Benefit:** "This approach will boost adoption rates, minimize disruptions, and keep us on track to achieve our efficiency goals."

What? So What? Now What?

- **What?** "Several departments are having difficulty with the new digital platform, resulting in inconsistent use and lower productivity."
- **So What?** "If these challenges persist, we risk delaying the overall rollout and failing to realize our projected efficiency improvements."
- **Now What?** "We'll address this by launching a tailored support program, including workshops and one-on-one coaching, to bring all teams up to speed."

Past–Present–Future:

- **Past:** "When we kicked off the digital transformation initiative last year, our goal was to streamline workflows and reduce manual errors."
- **Present:** "Today, while many teams are using the new system effectively, others are struggling with adoption, creating uneven results."
- **Future:** "Our next step is to provide enhanced training and change-management support to ensure all teams are fully equipped and aligned by the end of the next quarter."

This example demonstrates how you can utilize various structures to tailor the same core message to your audience's needs and the context of the conversation. Choosing the proper framework helps you deliver your message with clarity, focus, and persuasive impact, making it easier for your listeners to understand, remember, and act on your recommendations.

4. Ensure Non-Verbal Cues Align with Your Message

Communication is not only verbal. Tone of voice, facial expressions, and gestures carry immense weight in how your words are interpreted (Mehrabian, 1972; Pease & Pease, 2004). Even the clearest message can be undermined by mismatched delivery. Aligning these cues builds trust and clarity.

To align non-verbal cues with your message:

- Maintain an engaged and confident posture.
- Make consistent, friendly eye contact.
- Match your facial expression to your message (smile when positive).
- Modulate your tone for emphasis and warmth.

Example:

A manager might say, "I'm excited about this new initiative," while looking distracted and speaking in a monotone. The team senses disinterest, killing enthusiasm before it starts.

Non-verbal alignment is particularly crucial in cross-cultural communication, where gestures and expressions may carry different meanings. Practicing awareness and sensitivity can help avoid unintended misunderstandings.

Clarity is not about dumbing down your message. It's about respecting your audience enough to make your ideas accessible and actionable (Plain Language Action and Information Network, 2011). When you speak with clarity, you don't just share information, you build understanding, create alignment, and earn trust.

When you speak with clarity, you don't just share information, you build understanding. You create alignment. You earn trust. And you empower others to act with confidence and purpose.

By committing to these practical strategies, you will strengthen your professional impact, enhance your leadership, and cultivate a culture where communication drives results, not confusion. Clarity is not a luxury in professional life; it is a vital skill that transforms how you lead, collaborate, and achieve success.

Section 2: Empathy and Active Listening

Empathy is the foundation of meaningful, effective communication. It's the disciplined ability to set aside your assumptions and truly see the world through someone else's eyes, to understand their emotions, motivations, concerns, and unspoken needs. In professional settings, empathy goes far beyond simple kindness or courtesy. It's a critical strategic skill that strengthens leadership impact, supports high-performing, cohesive teams, and helps build resilient organizational cultures that can adapt and thrive in times of change (Brown, 2018; Covey, 2006).

At its core, empathy creates psychological safety, that vital sense of trust where people feel free to speak honestly without fear of ridicule, dismissal, or retaliation (Edmondson, 2019). When employees know they're heard and valued, they're far more likely to share ideas, raise concerns early, and engage in open, productive dialogue. This trust becomes the foundation of authentic relationships that transcend transactional interactions. It enables teams to collaborate more openly, manage conflict constructively, and stay aligned around shared goals, even under pressure.

But empathy on its own isn't enough. To truly have an impact, it must be paired with active listening, the disciplined practice of giving someone your full, undivided attention with the intention of understanding, not simply responding. Too often, professionals slip into the habit of "listening to respond," mentally preparing their counterarguments while the other person is still talking. By taking this approach, you lose valuable insights, engage in surface-level discussions, and create avoidable conflicts. Active listening requires us to slow down, set aside judgments, resist distractions, and fully focus on what's being said, and what's not.

Active listening also involves tuning in to emotional undercurrents. It means recognizing that words are only part of the message. Tone of voice, body language, pauses, hesitations, and silences can all reveal deeper feelings or concerns (Goleman, 2013; Pease & Pease, 2004). Effective communicators learn to pick up on these subtle cues and respond with empathy, asking thoughtful follow-up questions, reflecting back what they've heard to ensure understanding, or simply giving the speaker space and silence so they feel safe to elaborate further.

This section will explore why empathy and active listening are crucial to professional excellence and introduce practical, proven techniques to help you integrate them into your daily interactions. You'll learn tools such as reflective listening, open-ended questions, emotional labeling, and the power of supportive silence to transform even the most challenging conversations. We'll also explore the core principles of active listening in detail, showing how clarifying, reflecting, and allowing space can deepen understanding and build trust. By practicing these skills consistently, you'll create an environment where everyone feels respected, valued, and encouraged to contribute their best work.

Core Empathy Techniques

Empathy is more than a trait; it is a skill that is practiced and transforms the quality of our communication (Brown, 2018). At its core, empathy involves stepping beyond our viewpoint to truly understand and honor the experiences of others. In the workplace, where conversations are often fast-paced and outcome-driven, applying empathy requires intentionality. It asks us to pause, listen actively, and respond in ways that affirm both the content and the emotion behind what is being shared (Covey, 2006).

This section introduces four core techniques that serve as practical tools for expressing empathy in everyday professional interactions (See Figure 8). These methods are not only essential for building trust and emotional safety but also for fostering collaboration, reducing conflict, and strengthening interpersonal relationships. Whether you are navigating a difficult conversation, mentoring a colleague, or leading a diverse team, these techniques will equip you with the ability to connect more deeply and communicate with compassion and clarity.

Core Empathy Techniques

Empathy is more than a trait—it is a skill that is practiced and transforms the quality of our communication.

Reflective Listening
Paraphrasing or restating what the other person has said to demonstratè understanding

Open-Ended Inquiry
Asking questions that encourage the speaker to elaborate and share mure

Emotional Labeling
Identifying and naming the speaker's feelings to show recognition

Supportive Silence
Allowing pauses in conversation to give the speaker space to expresss themselves

Figure 8: Core Empathy Techniques

1. Reflective Listening

Reflective listening is the practice of paraphrasing or restating what another person has said to ensure mutual understanding and demonstrate genuine attention (Rogers & Farson, 1957). It signals respect, confirms accuracy, and helps prevent miscommunication.

During a team feedback session, a colleague says, "I feel like my ideas aren't considered in our planning meetings."
You respond:

"So what I'm hearing is that you feel your contributions haven't been taken seriously during planning sessions. Is that right?"

This approach gives the speaker a chance to affirm or correct the interpretation, creating a feedback loop that builds trust and clarity.

2. Open-Ended Inquiry

Open-ended questions invite deeper responses, reflection, and insight. They show curiosity and a willingness to understand beyond surface-level communication (Brown, 2018).

Instead of asking, "Did that meeting go well?" ask:

"What part of the meeting felt most productive for you?"

Or:

"How did the discussion about the new project affect your confidence in the team's direction?"

These types of questions allow space for elaboration and emotional nuance, uncovering motivations and concerns that might otherwise remain hidden.

3. Emotional Labeling

Emotional labeling means identifying and naming the feelings you perceive in others. This validates the speaker's emotions and shows that you are attuned to more than just their words; it reflects your emotional intelligence (Goleman, 2013).

A teammate has just vented about being assigned more work without notice. You say: "It sounds like you're feeling overwhelmed and maybe even unappreciated for the extra effort you are putting in."

When done correctly, emotional labeling diffuses tension and builds connection by showing empathy without judgment.

4. Supportive Silence

Supportive silence involves allowing natural pauses in conversation to create a safe space for more profound thought and emotional expression. It's the practice of "holding space" without rushing to fill every moment with words (Covey, 2006).

In a one-on-one check-in, an employee shares that they are having a tough time managing their workload. Instead of jumping in with a solution, you nod and stay quiet for a few seconds. The silence encourages them to continue:

"...and I guess I haven't told anyone how much it's been affecting me outside of work, too."

That extra space allowed a surface-level conversation to evolve into a more meaningful exchange.

Empathy isn't just about kindness; it's about competence. It strengthens collaboration, unlocks creativity, and enriches communication, making it richer and more human. When you listen with empathy, you lead with impact.

The Principle of Active Listening

Too often, professionals engage in "listening to respond" rather than "listening to understand" (Rogers & Farson, 1957). In these moments, people focus on crafting their rebuttal or pushing their agenda instead of truly absorbing what is being said. This habit prevents you from gaining valuable insights, weakens engagement, and can even create conflict. Active listening challenges us to slow down, set aside our assumptions, and focus entirely on the other person's perspective.

Active listening involves several professional behaviors:

- **Paying Full Attention**: eliminating distractions and maintaining eye contact or presence in virtual settings.
- **Demonstrating Attentiveness**: using verbal and non-verbal signals like nodding, leaning forward, and acknowledging understanding.
- **Clarifying Meaning**: asking questions to ensure you truly grasp what's being said.
- **Reflecting**: paraphrasing to confirm shared understanding and demonstrate respect.
- **Allowing Space**: using silence intentionally to encourage deeper sharing.

These techniques help ensure that the speaker feels heard, validated, and respected, which is essential for building trust and fostering open, productive conversations.

Active Listening in Practice

Active listening also means being attuned to emotional undercurrents. Often, what people say directly is only part of the message. Tone, body language, hesitation, and choice of words can reveal deeper feelings or unspoken concerns (Goleman, 2013; Pease & Pease, 2004). Effective communicators listen for these subtle cues and seek to clarify them with empathy.

This can mean asking gentle follow-up questions, reflecting what you heard, or simply allowing silence so the other person feels safe to elaborate (Covey, 2006).

Example scenario:

A team member says, "I'm not sure this approach will work."

A typical response might be defensive, "Of course it will!" which can shut down the dialogue.

An active listening response might be: "Can you tell me more about what concerns you?"

This simple, open-ended question signals respect and creates space for meaningful dialogue, transforming potential conflict into a collaborative effort.

Professional Value of Active Listening

Active listening is not a passive or "soft" skill; it is a deliberate, disciplined practice that enhances professional effectiveness in every role. It demonstrates respect for colleagues, improves problem-solving by surfacing real issues, and reduces costly misunderstandings. In leadership, active listening enables you to motivate teams, defuse conflict early, and build cultures of trust and inclusion.

Organizations that encourage active listening see tangible benefits:

- Higher employee engagement and retention.
- Stronger cross-functional collaboration.
- Fewer errors from miscommunication.
- Faster problem resolution and innovation.

Active listening also strengthens your professional brand. People are more likely to see you as approachable, credible, and trustworthy, qualities that open doors to new opportunities and leadership roles (Goleman, 2013).

Integrating Empathy and Active Listening

Empathy and active listening are not separate practices but mutually reinforcing. Empathy gives you the intention to understand and care about another's experience. Active listening gives you the method to do so skillfully and consistently. Together, they enable you to communicate in ways that go beyond exchanging information to building a real connection. Professionals who combine empathy and active listening:

- Ensure that people feel safe speaking honestly.
- Surface hidden challenges or opportunities.
- Strengthen alignment and buy-in.
- Foster relationships that endure change and stress.

They also model the behaviors they want to see in others, creating cultures where communication is respectful, thoughtful, and practical.

A Call to Practice

Like any skill, empathy and active listening require practice and reflection. You can start small:

- ✓ Pause before responding.
- ✓ Ask open-ended questions.
- ✓ Reflect back on what you hear.
- ✓ Pay attention to non-verbal cues.
- ✓ Acknowledge emotions without dismissing them.
- ✓ Embrace moments of silence.

Over time, these behaviors become habits that transform not just how you communicate but how you lead, collaborate, and build relationships. Empathy and active listening are not about avoiding conflict or always agreeing. They are about creating the conditions for honest, respectful dialogue, even when you disagree. By practicing them intentionally, you will improve your effectiveness while helping create workplaces where everyone feels heard, valued, and empowered to contribute (Edmondson, 2019).

In a world often characterized by rapid exchanges and surface-level engagement, dedicating the time to listen keenly and respond empathetically opens the door to profound professional relationships. Each conversation becomes an opportunity to learn, grow, and connect, not just as colleagues, but as human beings.

Through continued practice of these skills and a commitment to genuine communication, your capacity to influence positive outcomes in professional interactions will expand significantly. Embrace the journey, and let empathy guide the way to a more profound and impactful communication experience.

Empathy and Active Listening in Action: Emma's Story

Emma, a marketing manager, was known for her results-driven approach. Her campaigns were effective and on time. But her focus on outcomes often sidelined her team's input, leaving them disengaged.

During a tense planning meeting, Alex, one of her team members, voiced his frustration: "I don't think you're hearing us."

Instead of immediately defending herself, Emma paused. Remembering her commitment to active listening, she made eye contact and asked:

"Can you help me understand what's making you feel that way?"

That single question shifted the room. Alex explained how his ideas were often dismissed without discussion. Others shared similar experiences. Emma listened without interrupting, paraphrased their concerns, and acknowledged their feelings:

"I see how that's frustrating. I appreciate you sharing this."

This moment didn't just salvage the meeting; it transformed Emma's leadership style. Over time, she practiced routinely inviting input, clarifying understanding, and validating her team's perspectives. The result was greater trust, improved morale, and more creative, effective campaigns.

Section 3: Leveraging Non-Verbal Communication

In professional life, communication goes far beyond the words you speak or write. Non-verbal communication, the subtle but powerful signals you send through body language, facial expressions, tone of voice, eye contact, and even well-timed silences, is a critical, often decisive part of how you connect with others. Words provide information, but non-verbal cues reveal emotion and intent, while also building credibility. They shape not just what people hear but how they feel about what you say (Burgoon, Guerrero, & Floyd, 2016).

Mastering non-verbal communication is essential for anyone who wants to build trust, inspire confidence, and drive effective collaboration (Goleman, 2013). Think about the impact of a warm smile, steady and welcoming eye contact, an open, relaxed posture, or a calm, reassuring tone. These small behaviors send big messages about respect, authenticity, and approachability (Pease & Pease, 2004). They make people more willing to listen, share, and work with you. On the other hand, crossed arms, avoiding eye contact, distracted fidgeting, or a harsh tone can quickly erode trust, shut down conversation, and create barriers to understanding, even when your words are carefully chosen.

Non-verbal communication is especially critical in leadership roles. Leaders are always "on stage," with every gesture, glance, and tone conveying something about their priorities, values, and emotional state (Goleman, Boyatzis, & McKee, 2013). A leader's ability to project calm under pressure, to show genuine listening with attentive posture and eye contact, or to deliver feedback with a supportive tone has a direct impact on team morale, psychological safety, and overall performance (Edmondson, 2019). Similarly, in client meetings or negotiations, your body language and tone can mean the difference between building a strong relationship and damaging your credibility.

This section explains why non-verbal communication is crucial to professional success and offers practical strategies for using it intentionally. You'll learn to recognize and refine key elements, such as body language, facial expressions, and tone of voice, ensuring they support and enhance your spoken message to increase clarity, trust, and impact. We'll explore how aligning your words with your non-verbal signals builds credibility, while conflicting cues breed confusion and doubt. Through real-world examples, you'll see how even subtle changes in posture, gestures, eye contact, and tone can transform interactions, from one-on-one coaching sessions to high-stakes presentations.

Ultimately, using non-verbal communication effectively isn't about putting on a performance or manipulating people. It's about authentic alignment. It means ensuring that how you show up, in the room, on a call, or at the podium, truly reflects your values, intentions, and respect for your audience. By ensuring your non-verbal cues support your words, you create communication that is both clear and trustworthy.

Body Language: The Silent Language of Confidence and Engagement

Body language is often described as the "silent language" of communication because it conveys meaning without a single spoken word (Pease & Pease, 2004).

It encompasses posture, movement, gestures, and physical orientation, all of which work together to shape how others perceive us, how they interpret our messages, and how they respond to us (Knapp et al., 2013).

In professional settings, body language is powerful because it operates below conscious awareness. People instinctively read these signals to assess credibility, confidence, openness, and intent (Burgoon et al., 2016).

Even if you choose your words carefully, your body can still reveal hesitation or defensiveness if you're not mindful.

Mastering body language is not about performing or pretending. It is about aligning your physical presence with your message, ensuring consistency and authenticity so others can trust what you say and feel comfortable engaging with you (Goleman, 2013).

Below, we'll explore three critical elements of body language: posture, gestures, and movement/orientation, each with a comprehensive scenario to show how they work in practice.

1. Posture: Communicating Confidence and Openness

Posture is the foundation of body language. It reflects how you carry yourself in space, whether standing or sitting, and sends immediate cues about your confidence, approachability, and engagement.

- **Open posture** (standing tall, shoulders back, arms relaxed) signals confidence, readiness to engage, and accessibility.
- **Closed posture** (crossed arms, hunched shoulders, turned away) often signals defensiveness, insecurity, or resistance, even if unintended.

Because posture is so instinctive, even small changes can have a significant impact on how others perceive you.

Scenario: Team Kick-Off Meeting

Jasmine, a new project manager, is leading her first kickoff meeting with a cross-functional team. She knows the group is cautious about the project's tight timeline.

- ✓ Jasmine chooses to stand tall at the front of the room, feet firmly planted, shoulders back. She keeps her arms relaxed at her sides, using them naturally to gesture when speaking.

✓ When she invites questions, she leans forward slightly, signaling she's listening intently.

✓ She avoids crossing her arms or putting her hands in her pockets, which could signal impatience or disinterest.

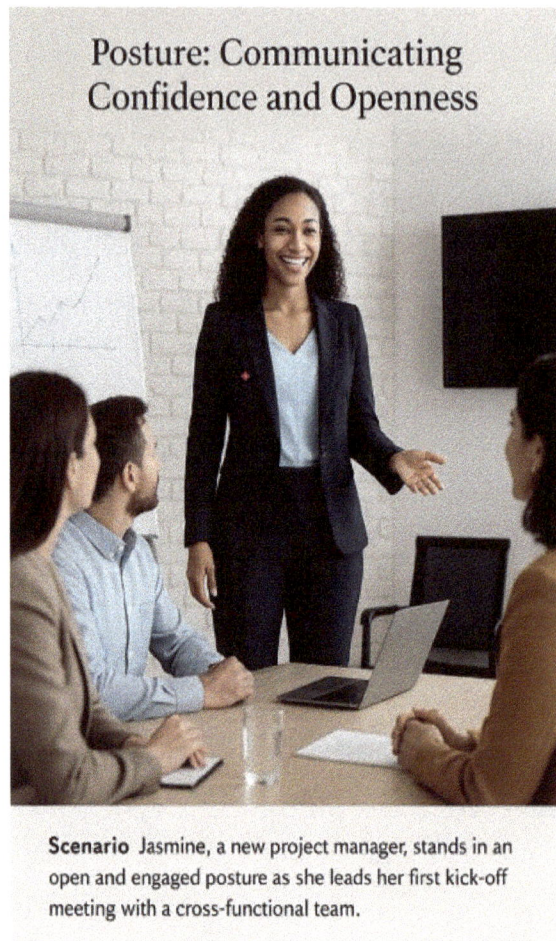

Posture: Communicating Confidence and Openness

Scenario Jasmine, a new project manager, stands in an open and engaged posture as she leads her first kick-off meeting with a cross-functional team.

As a result, the team perceives Jasmine as confident but approachable. Her open posture invites participation, reduces anxiety about the timeline, and sets a tone of collaboration. Team members are more willing to voice concerns early, helping Jasmine spot risks and manage them proactively.

2. Gestures: Reinforcing Your Message

Gestures are deliberate movements of the hands, arms, or head that reinforce what you're saying. Effective gestures can clarify meaning, emphasize key points, and keep your audience engaged.

- **Purposeful gestures** (open palms, illustrating size or direction) signal honesty, inclusion, and enthusiasm.
- **Distracting gestures** (fidgeting, pointing aggressively) can undermine credibility and distract from your message.

Gestures should be natural extensions of your words, not exaggerated performances.

Scenario: Client Pitch Presentation

Carlos, a business development lead, is pitching a new service package to a group of potential clients.

- ✓ As he describes the package's two core benefits, he counts them off with open, measured hand gestures.
- ✓ When explaining the integration with existing systems, he uses his hands to "show" how components connect, making abstract ideas more concrete.
- ✓ His palms remain open and visible, signaling transparency and welcoming questions.

He avoids fidgeting with a pen or clicking through slides too quickly. Instead, his controlled and intentional gestures amplify the clarity of his message while reinforcing the confidence behind it. The clients remain engaged throughout, asking thoughtful questions and ultimately expressing interest in moving forward.

3. Movement and Physical Orientation: Commanding Space with Purpose

How you move and orient yourself in a space reveals to others your confidence, authority, and engagement. Purposeful movement draws attention to key ideas, demonstrates comfort in your role, and invites collaboration.

- **Deliberate movement** (approaching a whiteboard, stepping closer to emphasize a point) shows you're in control and invested.
- **Restless movement** (pacing aimlessly, shifting weight repeatedly) can signal anxiety or lack of preparation.

Orientation matters, too: facing your audience squarely demonstrates openness, while turning away can suggest avoidance or dismissiveness.

Scenario: Strategy Workshop Facilitation

Ghadeer, an experienced facilitator, is leading an HR strategy workshop with a group of department heads.

- ✓ As the session begins, she stands slightly off-center rather than hiding behind a podium, signaling informality and openness.
- ✓ When summarizing group input on the whiteboard, she moves toward it deliberately, writes clearly, and then turns back to the group to maintain connection.
- ✓ During a critical discussion about priorities, she takes a single step closer to the table, leaning in slightly to emphasize the importance of alignment.
- ✓ She orients her body to face whoever is speaking, nodding gently to encourage participation.

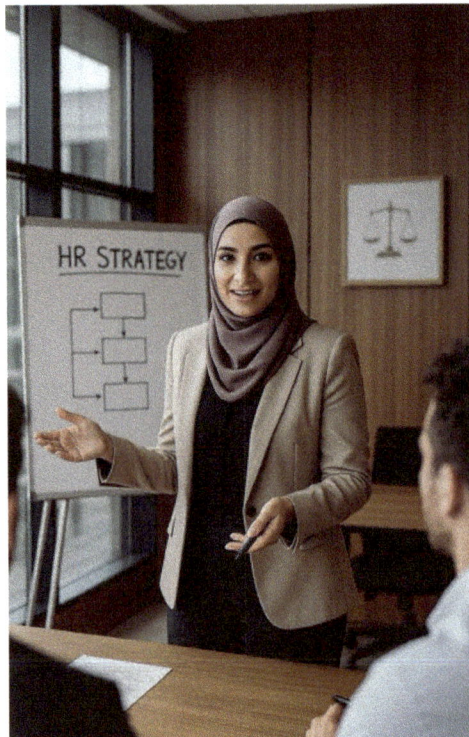

Throughout, Ghadeer avoids pacing or shifting from foot to foot unnecessarily. Her calm, intentional movement helps her command the room without coming across as authoritarian. Participants feel respected, engaged, and motivated to collaborate on solutions.

Body language is not an afterthought; it is a core part of how you communicate meaning, credibility, and respect. Mastering it means learning to use posture, gestures, and movement intentionally so they align with and amplify your message.

In every professional interaction, from a one-on-one check-in to a boardroom presentation, your body language sets the stage for how others perceive you and how effectively they will respond. By developing awareness and practicing purposeful behaviors, you will project confidence, foster trust, and elevate your communication from merely functional to powerfully impactful.

Facial Expression: The Gateway to Connection and Trust

Your face is one of the most powerful communication tools you have. Unlike words, facial expressions provide an immediate and universally understood window into one's emotional state and intentions (Ekman & Friesen, 1975). People instinctively watch your face for clues about whether you are sincere, engaged, empathetic, or distracted (Knapp et al., 2013).

In professional settings, facial expressions are essential for building trust, diffusing tension, and signaling that you are truly present. Even the most carefully crafted message can lose its impact if delivered with a mismatched or blank expression (Burgoon et al., 2016).

Mastering your facial expressions is not about pretending to feel emotions. It's about being intentional and congruent, ensuring that what you feel, intend, and say is genuinely reflected in your facial expression. This congruence lies at the heart of authentic communication and psychological safety in the workplace.

Key Elements of Effective Facial Expression

A Genuine Smile

A genuine smile, one that reaches the eyes, conveys warmth, trustworthiness, and approachability. It signals that you are open, positive, and ready to connect. Smiling can lower social tension, put others at ease, and make even difficult conversations feel more human and respectful. However, forced or insincere smiles are easy to spot and can breed distrust. Authenticity is key.

Eye Contact

Through eye contact, you convey attentiveness and sincerity while also demonstrating respect. Maintaining steady, appropriate eye contact signals that you are listening, engaged, and confident. It creates a sense of connection that words alone cannot achieve. However, eye contact should be balanced: too little can suggest insecurity or avoidance, while staring without breaks can be perceived as aggressive or uncomfortable.

Congruence

Congruence means ensuring that your facial expression matches your message. Mixed signals create confusion and erode trust. For example, delivering praise while frowning or discussing serious feedback while smirking sends conflicting messages that make others question your sincerity. Congruent expressions build alignment between what you say and how you say it, making your communication more transparent and more believable.

Scenario: One-on-One Performance Review

Maria is a department manager conducting a quarterly performance review with James, a valued team member who's performed well but needs to develop stronger client communication skills.

As James enters the room, Maria greets him with a genuine smile that immediately sets a warm, welcoming tone. This small gesture reduces any anxiety James may feel about the review.

Throughout the conversation, Maria maintains consistent eye contact, looking at James when he speaks, nodding gently to show she's listening. She avoids checking her phone or glancing at the clock, demonstrating full attention.

- ✓ When delivering positive feedback, Maria's facial expression is congruent. She smiles warmly and says, "Your project leadership this quarter was excellent. The team responded to your direction." Her expression matches her words, making the praise feel sincere and earned.
- ✓ When discussing areas for improvement, Maria adopts a more serious yet empathetic tone. She softens her eyes, lowers her voice slightly, and says: "One thing I'd like us to focus on is your communication with clients. Let's talk about strategies to make that even stronger."
- ✓ At key moments, Maria uses expressive listening cues, such as raising her eyebrows slightly when James shares an idea, nodding to show understanding, and smiling when he suggests an improvement plan.

QUARTERLY PERFORMANCE REVIEW

By aligning her facial expressions with the tone and content of the conversation, Maria fosters a safe and respectful environment. James experiences being heard and valued, which fuels his motivation to improve rather than feeling dismissed or criticized.

Facial expressions play a central role in emotional intelligence during communication. They help you:

- **Build Trust:** People believe what they see on your face more than what they hear in your words.
- **Enhance Connection:** Subtle cues, such as a smile or nod, make others feel seen and respected.
- **Manage Tension:** An empathetic, calm expression can de-escalate stressful conversations.
- **Signal Authenticity:** Congruent expressions show that you mean what you say.

In leadership, coaching, collaboration, or client relations, your facial expressions can mean the difference between connection and disconnection, trust and suspicion, progress and resistance.

Your face tells a story before you speak. By mastering the skill of aligning your expressions with your message, you invite trust, encourage openness, and foster professional relationships built on respect and understanding.

Whether offering feedback, negotiating with a client, or hearing a colleague's concerns, your facial expressions create connection and build trust. Use them wisely, intentionally, and authentically to strengthen your impact as a communicator and leader.

Tone of Voice: The Emotional Undercurrent of Communication

Your tone of voice is one of the most subtle yet powerful elements of professional communication. It is the emotional undercurrent that gives life and meaning to your words (Goleman, 2013). While your choice of words conveys content, your tone reveals attitude, emotion, and intent. It shapes not only what people hear but also how they interpret it, making the difference between sounding confident or uncertain, supportive or critical, engaged or indifferent (Knapp et al., 2013).

In professional settings, tone of voice is critical because it can reinforce or completely contradict your message. You might say, "I understand," but your tone can convey empathy, dismissiveness, sarcasm, or even impatience (Mehrabian, 1971). Professionals need to carefully consider their vocal delivery to ensure it supports their message and encourages trust, clarity, and collaboration.

Mastering tone of voice is not about scripted delivery. It's about purposeful variation, modulating pitch, pace, and volume to emphasize empathy, maintain interest, and inspire trust (Burgoon et al., 2016).

Key Elements of Tone of Voice

Warm, Modulated Tone

A warm, controlled tone projects calm, empathy, and approachability. It reassures listeners that you are thoughtful, balanced, and respectful. By modulating your tone, adjusting pitch, and pace, you show genuine engagement with the conversation.

Monotone Delivery

When your tone lacks variation, it can communicate disinterest, fatigue, or even a lack of enthusiasm. Even important ideas can sound dull or unconvincing when delivered in a monotonous manner. This risks disengaging your audience and making you appear disconnected from your message.

Strategic Modulation

Purposeful variation in pitch, pace, and volume adds emphasis and keeps your listener's attention. Speeding up can convey excitement or urgency; slowing down underscores importance. Changes in pitch and inflection help prevent misunderstandings and highlight critical points.

Scenario: Delivering Performance Feedback

Marcus is a team leader preparing for a one-on-one performance review with Priya, a high-performing but sometimes overly assertive team member. The goal is to recognize her strengths while encouraging her to collaborate more effectively.

✓ Marcus begins the conversation with a warm, calm tone, saying:

"Priya, I want to start by recognizing the dedication you've shown on our latest project."

His voice is steady and relaxed, signaling sincerity and putting Priya at ease.

✓ As he discusses areas for improvement, Marcus slows his pace slightly and lowers his volume to emphasize thoughtfulness:

"One thing I'd like us to work on is ensuring that everyone's ideas are heard during meetings."

This gentle delivery avoids sounding accusatory, reducing defensiveness.

✓ When outlining next steps, Marcus uses strategic modulation to maintain Priya's attention and convey optimism:

"I'm confident that with just a few adjustments, you'll help make our team discussions even more productive."

His tone rises slightly on the words "confident" and "productive," infusing them with encouragement and positivity. By controlling his tone throughout the conversation, Marcus ensures his feedback feels balanced, respectful, and supportive. Priya leaves the meeting motivated to improve rather than feeling criticized or demoralized.

Your tone of voice is a direct channel to your emotional intelligence. It helps you:

- **Build Rapport:** A friendly, measured tone creates trust and openness.
- **Manage Conflict:** Calm, steady delivery can de-escalate tense situations.
- **Maintain Engagement:** Varied inflection keeps attention focused.
- **Express Empathy:** Softening your voice signals understanding and care.
- **Demonstrate Confidence:** Controlled pace and volume convey authority and preparedness.

Tone of voice is more than a delivery tool; it's **an emotional amplifier**. It can elevate your message from mere words to a meaningful connection, turning instructions into inspiration and feedback into growth.

By becoming aware of and controlling your pitch, pace, volume, and inflection, you ensure your words are received as intended. This mastery of tone will help you communicate with clarity, empathy, and impact, strengthening your professional presence and deepening trust in every interaction.

By refining body language, facial expressions, and vocal tone, professionals can align their non-verbal signals with their verbal messages, enhancing clarity, trust, and influence across all forms of communication. These subtle, yet powerful cues often determine not just what is heard, but how it is remembered.

Tips for mastering non-verbal skills:

1. **Check Your Posture:** An Upright stance shows presence.
2. **Practice Controlled Gestures:** Reinforce your points clearly.
3. **Develop Eye Contact:** Use the triangle method to engage naturally.
4. **Use Vocal Variation:** Emphasize key points and soften where needed.
5. **Record and Review:** Observe yourself to identify areas for improvement.
6. **Seek Feedback:** Ask colleagues how your presence comes across.

Kareem, a mid-career operations manager in a global logistics firm, was highly competent but often overlooked for leadership roles. His peers described him as "technically solid" but lacking in executive presence. After receiving this feedback during a performance review, Kareem decided to actively work on improving his non-verbal communication. He sought the help of an executive coach to refine his presence during meetings and presentations.

How Kareem applied the six tips:

1. Check Your Posture

Kareem noticed in recorded meetings that he often slouched and leaned away from the table. This unintentionally conveyed disinterest. He trained himself to sit upright, with his shoulders squared and his body aligned. This change alone shifted how others perceived his authority in team discussions.

2. Practice Controlled Gestures

Previously, Kareem's hand gestures were either too exaggerated or nonexistent. His coach guided him to use purposeful, symmetrical gestures that aligned with his message, such as open palms when inviting discussion or steepled fingers when emphasizing a strategic point. This reinforced the clarity and intention of his communication.

3. Develop Eye Contact

Kareem struggled to maintain consistent eye contact during client presentations, often focusing on the slides instead of the people. He adopted the "triangle method": alternating gentle eye contact between individuals' left and right eyes and the bridge of their nose every few seconds. This helped him appear more engaged without seeming intense or rehearsed.

4. Use Vocal Variation

His monotone delivery was identified as a barrier to influence. Kareem honed his pitch, emphasis, and pause through practice. In one all-hands presentation, he deliberately slowed his speech for key points and raised his tone to foster collaboration. His team later remarked that he sounded much more dynamic and inspiring.

5. Record and Review

Kareem used his smartphone to record weekly progress updates he gave to his team. Watching himself helped him identify distracting habits, such as fidgeting and a flat tone. Over time, the recordings revealed a marked improvement in confidence, clarity, and energy.

6. Seek Feedback

He invited a trusted colleague to observe him during a board presentation. She noted that while his content was strong, his pacing and posture made him appear rushed. Incorporating her feedback, Kareem adjusted his rhythm, grounded himself physically, and received praise for his calm and commanding presence in the next session.

Kareem's professional presence evolved significantly over six months. He became more impactful in meetings, gained trust from leadership, and was soon tasked with leading a high-visibility regional project. The difference wasn't just in his verbal communication; it was how his presence now complemented his message.

Non-verbal cues don't work in isolation; they amplify, support, or undermine your verbal message. When your words and non-verbal signals are aligned, you project authenticity, credibility, and confidence. But when they conflict, like praising someone while frowning or saying you're calm while your voice shakes, you create doubt and confusion.

Effective communicators learn to align posture, gestures, eye contact, facial expressions, and tone of voice with their words. This alignment fosters trust, minimizes misunderstandings, and ensures your message is conveyed as intended (Burgoon et al., 2016).

Mastering non-verbal communication isn't about performing tricks; it's about developing awareness, practicing consistently, and aligning how you show up with what you truly intend (Goleman, 2013). This takes time and reflection, but the impact is profound. You'll project confidence, foster trust, and engage others more deeply in every professional interaction.

By refining body language, facial expressions, and vocal tone, you ensure that your communication is not just heard but felt, and remembered (Knapp et al., 2013).

True communication mastery combines the outer tools, clarity, structure, tone, with the inner qualities, presence, empathy, and authenticity. When you align your message with who you are and how you carry yourself, your communication becomes a compelling force for connection, leadership, and impact.

Executive Snapshot – Chapter 2: Communication Mastery

Communication Mastery turns internal clarity into external influence. You learned to start with the audience's 'why', to listen actively for unmet needs, and to align verbal, written, and non-verbal signals. Intentional communication isn't about eloquence alone; it's about outcome alignment and relational trust. The summary below distils the high-leverage practices that convert messages into moments of shared understanding.

✓ Begin with the audience's 'why' to craft clear, outcome-based messages.
✓ Use active listening cues (paraphrasing, open questions) to build empathy.
✓ Align verbal, non-verbal, and written signals for credibility.
✓ Ask strategic questions to surface hidden assumptions and insights.
✓ Deliver feedback using the 'SBI-plus-future' model for growth-oriented conversations.
✓ Simplify language: one idea per sentence; max 22 words on average.

Reflection Question: Before your next high-stakes conversation, what clarity checkpoint will you use to confirm your message landed?

Chapter Three: Growth Orientation

In today's rapidly changing professional landscape, one truth is undeniable: the skills and knowledge that brought you success yesterday will not be enough for tomorrow. Growth is no longer optional. It is the foundation that helps you stay relevant and fulfilled in your career.

Importantly, growth orientation is not about blindly chasing every new trend or collecting credentials for their own sake. It is about adopting a professional stance that is relentlessly curious, deeply reflective, and firmly committed to deliberate, ongoing improvement. By taking this approach, you don't simply adapt to changes in your industry; you help shape them. You don't just protect your career; you expand its potential and increase your impact.

This chapter is organized around three essential dimensions of professional excellence:

First, adopting a growth mindset will help you make the mental shift needed for sustainable development. You'll explore the differences between fixed and growth mindsets and discover practical strategies to reframe setbacks as opportunities, stay motivated over the long term, and view challenges as essential parts of personal and professional growth. Embracing the growth mindset empowers you to pursue excellence with curiosity, humility, and determination.

Second, embracing lifelong learning demonstrates the importance of continuous and intentional development throughout your entire career. You'll examine different ways to learn, from formal education and certifications to informal exploration and hands-on experience. This section includes real stories of professionals who transformed their careers by cultivating curiosity and committing to learning every day. Reflection prompts will help you clarify your own learning goals and design a plan tailored to your needs.

Third, seeking and using feedback shows how feedback, from mentors, colleagues, and self-reflection, can become one of your most valuable growth tools. You'll learn how to create a clear, actionable personal learning plan, set SMART goals, choose the right resources, and maintain accountability through effective feedback loops.

Throughout this chapter, you'll find practical strategies, reflection exercises, and real-world examples that bring these ideas to life. This is not abstract theory; it is a hands-on guide to help you build what may be the most vital professional capability of all: the ability to keep growing, learning, and improving every single day.

Section 1: Cultivating a Growth Mindset

In today's rapidly changing professional world, staying stagnant isn't an option. Technology evolves at a rapid pace, industries shift, and customer expectations continue to grow. For professionals committed to growth orientation, this isn't something to fear but an opportunity to unlock their greatest potential (Dweck, 2006). Growth orientation is the deliberate practice of developing yourself over time. At its core lies a defining mindset: the growth mindset.

A growth mindset is the belief that abilities, intelligence, and skills can be strengthened through effort, feedback, and learning (Dweck, 2006). This isn't just a motivational slogan. It's a research-based approach that changes how we perceive challenges, accept feedback, and understand our capacity for improvement (Claro, Paunesku, & Dweck, 2016). Professionals with a growth mindset don't avoid new responsibilities or fear making mistakes. Instead, they embrace them, treating every experience as an opportunity to improve and deliver more value (Yeager & Dweck, 2020).

Growth orientation pushes us to let go of static thinking. A fixed mindset says, "I'm just not good at this," and closes the door to growth. A growth mindset reframes it: "I haven't mastered this yet, but I can with practice" (Dweck, 2006). This subtle shift encourages professionals to see learning as a lifelong journey, adapt to change, and remain relevant regardless of industry shifts. It also builds curiosity, humility, and resilience, qualities that underpin excellence throughout a career.

But a growth mindset isn't only about personal development. It is vital for teamwork and leadership. Professionals who embrace it are more open to feedback, collaborate more freely, and support the growth of colleagues (Heslin & Keating, 2017). Leaders who model a growth mindset foster cultures of learning and experimentation, where mistakes aren't punished but seen as opportunities. In this way, growth orientation becomes a shared advantage, helping teams continuously improve and succeed together (Dragoni et al., 2009).

This section explores why developing a growth mindset is essential for professional excellence. Adopting this mindset reshapes how you view learning, feedback, and failure, setting the stage for long-term success in any role. You'll also learn practical ways to turn this mindset into a habit you practice every day. By embracing this approach, you'll prepare yourself to lead with confidence, learn continuously, and deliver real value in a world that never stands still.

Fixed vs. Growth Mindset: A Foundational Shift

One of the most essential concepts in developing professional growth orientation is understanding the difference between a fixed mindset and a growth mindset, a distinction popularized by psychologist Carol Dweck (2006). This shift isn't just motivational, it's transformative.

What is a Fixed Mindset?

Fixed-mindset professionals believe intelligence, talents, and abilities are innate and unchangeable. They avoid challenges to protect their self-image, fear making mistakes, view effort as proof of inadequacy, and resist feedback, perceiving it as criticism. Because of this belief:

- They **avoid challenges**, fearing failure will expose their limitations.
- They **fear mistakes** because errors are interpreted as evidence of inadequacy.
- They see **effort** as a sign they lack talent, thinking, "If I have to try this hard, I must not be good at it."
- They **resist feedback**, viewing it as criticism to be defended against, not an opportunity to improve.

A professional with a fixed mindset might say:

"I'm terrible at public speaking, so I just avoid those opportunities."

Or:

"I'm not a tech person, so I won't even try to learn this new software."

These attitudes limit growth. By avoiding new experiences or skills, professionals with a fixed mindset miss out on opportunities for advancement, collaboration, and innovation. Their careers can stall, not because they lack talent, but because they limit their potential for growth and development.

What is a Growth Mindset?

In contrast, a **growth mindset** is the belief that intelligence and abilities can be developed over time through effort, learning, and feedback. Professionals with this mindset see their skills as dynamic, capable of improvement and refinement. This belief changes their entire approach:

- They **embrace challenges** as opportunities to learn and grow.
- They see **effort** as essential and valuable, a sign they're investing in themselves.
- They **view mistakes** not as failures, but as vital feedback about what to improve.
- They **actively seek feedback** to gain new perspectives and accelerate learning.

A professional with a growth mindset might say:

"Presenting makes me nervous, but I know I can get better if I practice and get feedback."

Or:

"I'm not familiar with this new system yet, but I'll take the training and ask questions until I'm confident."

Professionals with a growth mindset are more adaptable, collaborative, and resilient (Yeager & Dweck, 2020).

Why This Shift Matters Professionally

The difference between these mindsets is not theoretical; it has profound real-world consequences in professional life:

- **Career Development:** Professionals with a growth mindset are more likely to seek new roles, responsibilities, and learning opportunities. Those with a fixed mindset often play it safe and stagnate.
- **Teamwork:** Growth-minded professionals value others' perspectives and feedback, making them better collaborators. Fixed-mindset colleagues may be defensive or dismissive.
- **Resilience:** When projects fail or markets shift, growth-minded professionals see it as a learning experience. Fixed-minded professionals may feel defeated or blame others.
- **Leadership:** Leaders with a growth mindset encourage learning and experimentation within their teams. They create environments where people feel safe taking risks and growing.

The Reframing at the Heart of Growth

Ultimately, a growth mindset reframes the very purpose of work and learning. Instead of trying to prove your worth by avoiding mistakes and protecting your ego, you focus on developing your worth through continual improvement.

- **Fixed Mindset Purpose:** Prove you're good enough.
- **Growth Mindset Purpose:** Become better every day.

It's a shift from seeing mistakes as evidence you don't belong to seeing them as the most direct route to mastery. It's about cultivating curiosity, humility, and resilience, the core ingredients of professional adaptability.

By adopting a growth mindset, you position yourself not just to survive change but to thrive in it, becoming the kind of professional who leads, learns, and drives progress in any environment.

Strategies to Cultivate a Growth Mindset

Cultivating a growth mindset is not as simple as deciding to "think positively" or adopting an optimistic attitude. It is a deliberate, ongoing practice that requires intentional effort, self-awareness, and consistent reinforcement.

Adaptability isn't something professionals stumble upon. It's cultivated through consistent habits and reflective practices that reshape how they approach challenges, setbacks, and learning.

Below are practical strategies to help you strengthen a growth mindset and integrate adaptability into your daily work. These approaches are designed not only to shift thinking but also to change behavior in a sustainable and meaningful way.

1. Reframe Setbacks as Learning Opportunities

A hallmark of a fixed mindset is interpreting setbacks as evidence of inadequacy or failure. In contrast, a growth mindset sees setbacks as essential learning moments, valuable data that guides improvement.

How to Practice It:

- When something doesn't go as planned, pause and reflect instead of blaming yourself or others.
- Ask yourself powerful, learning-focused questions:
  - "What did this experience teach me?"
  - "How will I approach this differently next time?"
  - "What signals did I miss, and how can I notice them earlier?"

Imagine you present a proposal that's rejected by senior leadership. A fixed-mindset response might be:

"I'm not good at presenting ideas. I'll avoid it next time."

A growth-minded approach would involve gathering feedback to understand why it didn't land, refining the message, and trying again with new insights.

"I didn't clearly show the ROI they needed to see. Next time, I'll focus on those numbers early in the presentation."

This approach transforms failure into a springboard for competence and confidence. Over time, you develop resilience, strategic thinking, and credibility as someone who continually learns and improves.

2. Celebrate Effort, Not Just Outcomes

In many professional environments, success is often measured solely by results. While outcomes are important, overemphasizing them can discourage experimentation and risk-taking. A growth mindset values the learning journey, recognizing that sustained effort is what ultimately leads to meaningful results over time.

How to Practice It:

- Regularly acknowledge and praise the process, not just the final product.
- Look for and highlight:
  - Initiative in tackling challenging tasks.
  - Persistence despite obstacles.
  - Creative problem-solving and experimentation.
- Reinforce the idea that learning happens in the doing, even when outcomes are imperfect.

A team member volunteers to lead a new, complex client project. The final deliverable has room for improvement, but their commitment and willingness to learn on the fly are invaluable.

A fixed-mindset response might focus solely on critique:

"You didn't get everything right."

A growth-minded leader would say:

"I appreciate you stepping up to lead. Let's review what went well and what we can improve for next time."

This approach nurtures a culture of psychological safety, motivating people to expand their capabilities, innovate, and acquire new skills, essential ingredients for adaptability in any organization.

3. Use Growth-Oriented Language

Our language reflects and reinforces our beliefs. The way we talk to ourselves (and others) can either lock us into a fixed mindset or open us up to growth. Small shifts in wording can significantly reshape attitudes and behaviors.

How to Practice It:

- Become aware of limiting self-talk that suggests abilities are fixed.
  - Examples: "I'm just not good at this." or "I'll never understand this."
- Replace it with growth-oriented alternatives that emphasize learning and progress.
  - "I'm still learning this skill."
  - "I haven't mastered this yet, but I can improve with practice."
  - "I can ask for help or resources to get better."

Instead of saying:

"I'm terrible at data analysis."

Try:

"I'm still learning how to analyze data effectively."

This small shift breaks down self-imposed barriers to growth, sparks curiosity, and fosters persistence. It shows both to others and to yourself that you are committed to evolving over time.

Cultivating a growth mindset is an intentional professional discipline. By reframing setbacks, celebrating effort, and using growth-oriented language, professionals don't just think differently, they act differently. With this mindset, challenges become opportunities, lifelong learning is fueled, and resilience is built for enduring success in a dynamic world.

The Mindset Builder Toolkit: Turning Growth into Daily Practice

Developing a growth mindset isn't a one-time decision; it's an ongoing commitment to seeing challenges, feedback, and effort as opportunities for learning and improvement. While the concept sounds inspiring, professionals often ask:

"How do I make this part of my daily work life?"

The answer lies in structured, practical tools that make growth-mindset behaviors habitual. By incorporating these simple yet powerful practices into your routine, you create an environment that fosters adaptability, emotional resilience, and ongoing development, especially in demanding, high-pressure roles.

Figure 9 shows the Mindset Builder Toolkit, designed to help you move from a growth mindset theory to everyday action.

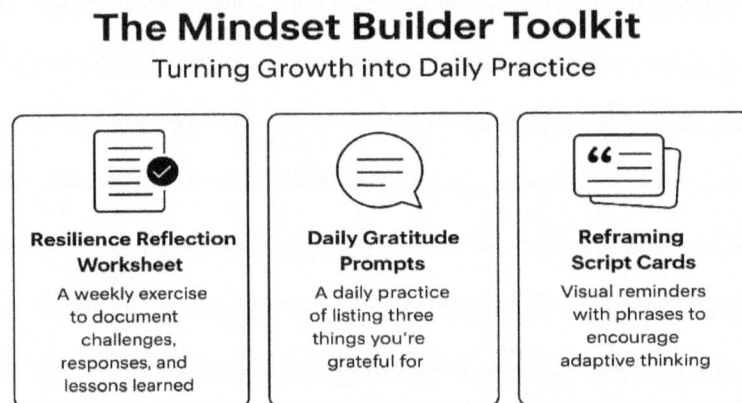

The Mindset Builder Toolkit
Turning Growth into Daily Practice

Resilience Reflection Worksheet	**Daily Gratitude Prompts**	**Reframing Script Cards**
A weekly exercise to document challenges, responses, and lessons learned	A daily practice of listing three things you're grateful for	Visual reminders with phrases to encourage adaptive thinking

Figure 9: The Mindset Builder Toolkit

1. Resilience Reflection Worksheet

What It Is:

A simple weekly exercise where you document:

- Challenges faced
- Your responses
- Lessons learned

Why It Works:

Most professionals experience setbacks but rush past them without meaningful reflection. This habit can reinforce avoidance or self-criticism. The worksheet normalizes setbacks as integral to growth by creating a structured space to analyze them without judgment.

How to Use It:

- Set aside 10–15 minutes at the end of each week.
- Write down specific challenges, no matter how big or small.
- Reflect on how you responded, both what went well and what could improve.
- Capture clear lessons to guide future actions.

Example:

Maria, a sales manager, was frustrated after losing a key client. Instead of ignoring it, she used the worksheet:

- **Challenge:** Lost a long-term client after a pricing negotiation.
- **Response:** Felt defensive and inflexible during the call.
- **Lesson:** Recognize early signs of tension. Prepare alternative solutions and practice active listening.

As a result, Maria prepared role-play sessions with her team to handle objections with empathy, improving overall negotiation outcomes in the next quarter.

2. Daily Gratitude Prompts

What It Is:

A short, daily practice of listing three things you're grateful for, from significant achievements to small moments of kindness or beauty.

Why It Works:

Gratitude is far from being just a pleasant sentiment. It's a proven strategy that builds emotional resilience, helps shift away from negative thinking, and keeps you focused during tough times. For busy professionals, it serves as a daily reset, helping balance stress with an appreciation of the positives.

How to Use It:

- Choose a consistent time, such as the start of the day, before bed, or during lunch.
- Write down three things you're grateful for.
- Aim for variety: include personal, professional, and even small sensory experiences.

Example:

Jamal, a product lead juggling a high-pressure launch, felt increasingly stressed and short-tempered. He began his day with gratitude prompts:

1. My team's dedication even during extended hours.

2. A helpful client who shared clear feedback.

3. Morning coffee ritual that grounds me.

Within weeks, Jamal noticed that he approached setbacks with greater calm, supported his team with increased empathy, and felt more connected to his purpose.

3. Reframing Script Cards

What It Is:

Visual reminders placed in your workspace feature growth-oriented language that encourages adaptive thinking in real-time.

Why It Works:

Stressful moments can trigger old, limiting self-talk:

"I'm not good at this."

"This feedback is personal."

Reframing cards disrupt these automatic responses, providing quick and accessible prompts to shift perspective immediately.

How to Use It:

- Write or print phrases on cards or sticky notes.
- Place them where you'll see them, on a monitor, notebook, or desk wall.
- Choose phrases that resonate with your challenges.

Example Phrases:

"I haven't mastered this yet."

"Feedback is data, not a personal attack."

"Challenges are opportunities to learn."

Example:

Elena, a senior project manager, struggled with defensive reactions during client feedback sessions. She placed a card on her monitor reading:

"Feedback is data, not a personal attack."

Seeing it before meetings helped her approach discussions with curiosity rather than fear. Over time, her ability to calmly ask clarifying questions and propose solutions transformed her client relationships and her reputation as a collaborative partner.

Adaptability is not just a response to change; it is a proactive approach to achieving professional excellence. At its core lies the **growth mindset**: the belief that skills can be developed, challenges are opportunities, and learning is a lifelong practice.

By intentionally cultivating this mindset, you don't just survive change, you lead through it with confidence, creativity, and impact.

Section 2: The Imperative of Lifelong Learning

In today's fast-paced, constantly evolving professional world, staying where you are isn't just risky, it's unsustainable. Technology advances quickly, industries shift direction seemingly overnight, and client expectations continually change. In this environment, lifelong learning isn't just a nice advantage to have; it's the essential foundation for staying relevant, successful, and resilient over the long term (Illeris, 2018; Senge, 2006).

Embracing lifelong learning means committing to ongoing, intentional growth. It is adopting a mindset that recognizes development doesn't have a finish line. Unlike a single degree or certification you earn and then consider "done," lifelong learning is about staying curious, adaptable, and open to new ideas throughout your entire career (Eraut, 2004; Kolb, 2015). This mindset is what distinguishes professionals who can adapt and thrive from those who risk falling behind.

Lifelong learning is unique to each individual. It involves recognizing your evolving goals and shaping your development to align with them. It includes formal education, which offers recognized credentials and structured knowledge; informal learning, which keeps you responsive to emerging ideas and best practices; and experiential learning, which deepens expertise and sharpens judgment through real-world problem-solving (Illeris, 2018; Marsick & Watkins, 2015). Each of these approaches makes a unique contribution to your ability to innovate, lead, and deliver meaningful results in your field.

This section is designed to help you view learning not as a box to check or a single event to complete, but as a dynamic, ongoing process that becomes an integral part of your professional identity. You'll explore how to integrate learning into your daily routines and long-term plans, building the resilience to handle uncertainty, the confidence to take on new challenges, and the capability to remain not just employable but truly indispensable.

You'll also encounter real-life stories of professionals who transformed their careers by adopting a learning mindset. Their journeys show that true learning isn't about collecting certificates or chasing the latest trends blindly; it's about cultivating curiosity, humility, and the drive to evolve in ways that are meaningful and strategic.

Ultimately, this section will offer practical guidance and structured tools to help you reflect on your own learning needs, identify areas for growth, and develop a personalized plan aligned with your career goals and aspirations. By prioritizing lifelong learning, you not only ensure your future but also discover new ways to experience fulfillment, adaptability, and impact.

As you move through this section, challenge yourself to see learning not as an obligation but as an investment in your most valuable asset: yourself. By embracing lifelong learning with purpose and enthusiasm, you'll build a career that is not only successful but deeply rewarding, resilient in the face of change, and genuinely aligned with your values and ambitions.

Three Modes of Lifelong Learning

Professional learning doesn't look the same for everyone, and it shouldn't. The most effective professionals blend three complementary learning modes to create a dynamic, personalized approach (See Figure 10).

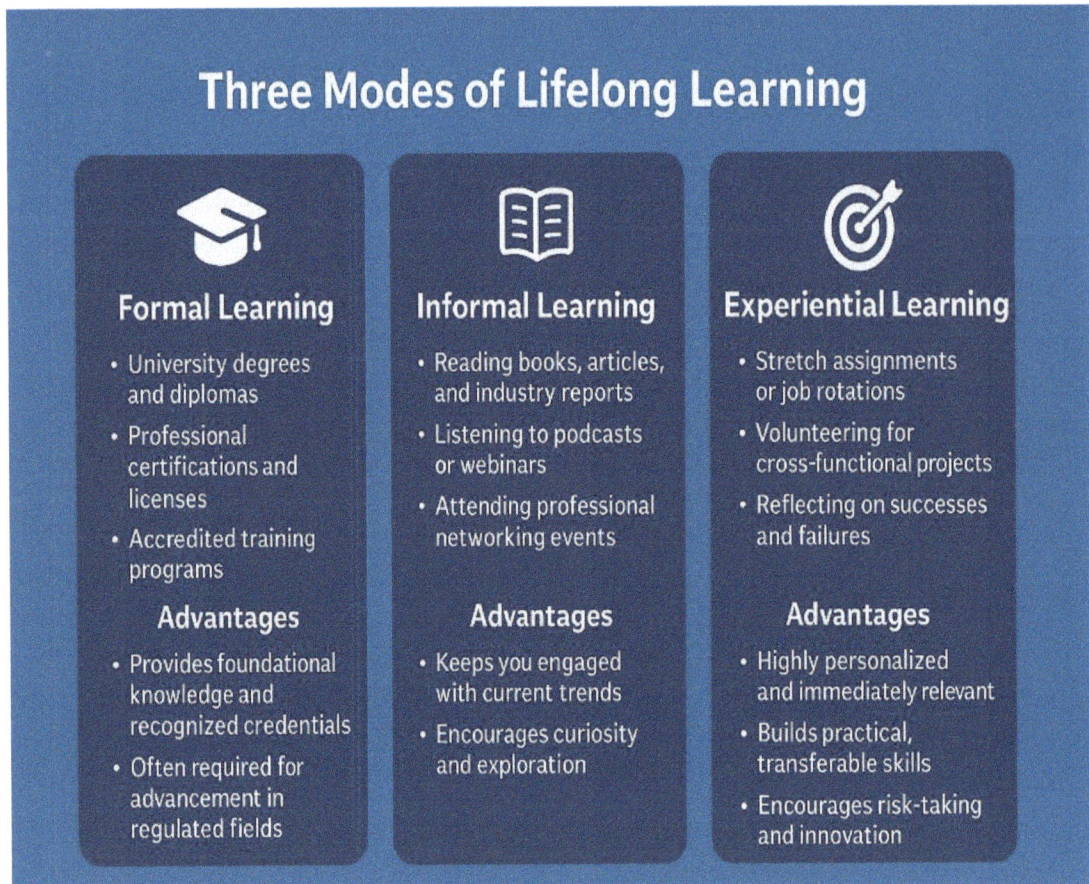

Figure 10: Three complementary modes of lifelong learning

1. Formal Learning

This includes structured, credentialed education:

- University degrees and diplomas.
- Professional certifications and licenses.
- Accredited training programs.

Advantages:

- Provides foundational knowledge and recognized credentials.
- Signals credibility to employers and clients.
- Often being required for advancement in regulated fields (Eraut, 2004).

Example:

An HR manager is pursuing a CIPD certification to deepen strategic HR knowledge and improve promotion prospects.

Formal learning provides structure and credibility. It delivers recognized credentials that can open doors to new roles, promotions, or opportunities in other industries. By earning certifications and degrees, you signal to employers, clients, and peers that you've invested in acquiring deep, validated knowledge. Formal education provides a solid grounding in theory, frameworks, and best practices, laying the groundwork for more flexible skills."

2. Informal Learning

Learning outside the classroom, self-directed and flexible:

- Reading books, articles, and industry reports.
- Listening to podcasts or webinars.
- Attending professional networking events.
- Conversations with peers and mentors.

Advantages:

- Keeps you engaged with current trends.
- Encourages curiosity and exploration.
- Being easy to integrate into daily routines (Brookfield, 2017)

Example:

A marketing specialist listens to digital strategy podcasts during commutes to stay ahead of industry shifts.

Informal learning keeps curiosity alive and ensures you stay connected to emerging trends, industry developments, and fresh ideas. Informal learning is self-directed and flexible, occurring daily through activities like reading, listening to podcasts, attending webinars, and engaging in meaningful conversations with peers and mentors. It allows you to explore new interests at your own pace, fill knowledge gaps in real time, and stay mentally agile in the face of change.

3. Experiential Learning

Learning by doing:

- Stretch assignments or job rotations.
- Volunteering for cross-functional projects.
- Reflecting on successes and failures.
- Maintaining a learning journal to capture insights.

Advantages:

- Highly personalized and immediately relevant.
- Builds practical, transferable skills.
- Encouraging risk-taking and innovation (Kolb, 2015)

Example:

An engineer volunteering for an AI integration project to learn cutting-edge technology hands-on.

Experiential learning takes development one step further by turning knowledge into action. This is where you learn by doing, through stretch assignments, cross-functional projects, volunteering for new responsibilities, or even learning from failures. Experiential learning is often the most personal and transformative because it requires you to apply knowledge, adapt in real-world conditions, reflect on outcomes, and iterate your approach. It develops practical, transferable skills that theory alone cannot teach.

Combining the Modes of Lifelong Learning

Each learning mode, from formal to informal to experiential, has its value, but professional mastery is found in blending them into a focused, intentional strategy (Senge, 2006). The most effective, agile professionals recognize that no single approach is sufficient on its own. Instead, they blend all three, creating a dynamic and resilient foundation for growth that evolves with their goals, industry demands, and personal interests.

Professionals who integrate these modes strategically gain significant advantages:

- **Depth and Credibility:** Formal education builds the foundational expertise and credentials necessary for career progression.
- **Breadth and Agility:** Informal learning keeps you adaptable, aware of new developments, and open to change.
- **Practical Mastery:** Experiential learning enables you to translate knowledge into impact, developing problem-solving skills, leadership abilities, and the confidence to tackle complex challenges.

For instance, imagine an HR professional seeking to drive organizational transformation:

- Earn a formal certification in change management to gain proven frameworks and industry credibility.
- Follow leading HR podcasts, read articles on evolving workforce trends, and attend industry conferences to stay informed about new ideas.
- Volunteer to lead a pilot change initiative in their organization, applying what they've learned, gaining firsthand experience, and refining their approach through reflection and feedback.

Similarly, a software engineer might:

- Pursue an advanced degree or certification in data science.
- Stay current by reading industry blogs, contributing to online forums, or watching expert talks.
- Join an internal innovation lab to prototype new solutions, learning through experimentation and collaboration.

By combining these modes, professionals develop rich and adaptable skill sets, as well as a future-ready mindset. This approach shapes a professional identity that grows, highlighting a commitment to continuous improvement, curiosity, and tangible impact, qualities that both employers value and clients admire.

Reflection: Charting Your Lifelong Learning Journey

Lifelong learning doesn't happen by accident; it begins with self-awareness and intentional reflection (Brookfield, 2017). Before designing a learning plan, you need clarity about your current situation, goals, and barriers.

Reflection is a powerful tool for clarifying your goals and mapping a meaningful path forward. It helps you identify strengths to build upon, gaps to address, and interests that can reignite your sense of purpose. By asking the right questions, you create a personal roadmap that turns vague ambition into actionable next steps.

Here are some guiding questions to help you begin this process:

1. Which aspects of my current role do I find most rewarding, and where do I feel less confident?

Identifying what energizes you can reveal your core strengths and values, while acknowledging areas of discomfort or insecurity highlights growth opportunities.

2. What emerging trends, technologies, or skills are shaping my industry?

Staying aware of industry shifts ensures that you remain relevant and proactive, rather than reactive. This question helps you prioritize learning that aligns with future opportunities.

3. Are there passions or interests I've put aside that could enrich my professional work?

Sometimes, the most meaningful learning comes from revisiting sidelined interests that can add depth, creativity, and satisfaction to your career.

4. Who in my network can serve as a mentor, coach, or source of inspiration?

Growth rarely happens in isolation. Identifying people who can offer guidance, feedback, or new perspectives is essential to your development.

5. What learning opportunities exist in my organization, industry, or community that I can leverage?

From internal training programs to professional groups and conferences, being aware of available resources empowers you to take action without delay.

Write down your reflections on these questions. Don't rush the process. Use your answers to clarify your goals and plan your next steps, whether that means enrolling in a course, seeking out mentorship, joining a new professional community, or volunteering for a challenging project that pushes you to grow.

A Reflective Case Study: Ghassan's Story

To see how this reflective process can transform a career, consider the story of Ghassan, a 55-year-old technology consultant who found himself at a crossroads. Though Ghassan had built a strong track record over 20 years of leading complex projects, he realized his motivation was fading. He felt stuck, unchallenged, and uncertain about his future direction.

Instead of ignoring these feelings or jumping impulsively into any new trend, Ghassan chose to pause and reflect intentionally on what he truly wanted from his professional journey.

Through structured reflection, Ghassan identified key insights and took targeted action:

- He realized he felt most energized during collaborative strategy sessions but lacked confidence in public speaking and written communication. To address this, he enrolled in a storytelling workshop and began publishing regular insights on LinkedIn to build his voice and credibility.
- He acknowledged a blind spot in understanding AI and its growing impact on consulting. Ghassan registered for an ethical AI course and joined his firm's internal think tank to learn from colleagues and explore practical applications.
- He wanted to connect his work to sustainability, an interest he had long set aside. Ghassan proposed an internal innovation initiative for a green technology advisory service, aligning personal passion with organizational strategy.
- Recognizing the need for a fresh perspective and accountability, he reached out to a former client who had transitioned to running a purpose-driven startup. Their coffee meeting evolved into a recurring mentorship relationship, helping Ghassan think more entrepreneurially about his career.
- Finally, Ghassan applied for and was accepted into a global leadership exchange program, which gave him access to new markets, diverse peers, and cross-industry insights.

Outcome

Within a year, Ghassan had completely redefined his professional identity. He wasn't simply following the latest industry trend or adding certifications without purpose. Instead, he aligned his learning with his values, strengths, and aspirations. He reignited his motivation, expanded his network, and positioned himself as an innovator within his firm.

Lifelong learning is not about endlessly consuming information or chasing every new trend. It is about intentionally shaping who you become as a professional. It requires self-awareness, curiosity, and the willingness to act on your insights.

Through formal education for foundational knowledge, informal learning for continuous adaptability, and experiential learning for practical mastery, along with goal reflection, you don't just build a career. You create a meaningful professional journey that evolves with you.

Embrace reflection as the starting point of this journey. It is the first, and most critical, step toward becoming not just prepared for change, but ready to lead it.

Creating a Personal Learning Plan

Embracing lifelong learning is more than simply valuing education or staying curious; it is about making learning an intentional, structured part of your professional journey. While curiosity fuels exploration and adaptability keep you open to change, it is planning that turns these mindsets into sustained growth (Marsick & Watkins, 2015).

A Personal Learning Plan is the practical foundation for lifelong learning. It helps you move from vague ambition, "I should learn more" to focused, strategic action that aligns with your goals, values, and evolving industry demands. Instead of reacting to change at the last minute, you proactively prepare yourself to grow in ways that matter.

Creating your learning plan begins with an important recognition: continuous learning isn't a choice, it's a necessity. The world of work is moving fast. Technology evolves, customer expectations shift, and industries transform. Professionals who thrive are those who can navigate this complexity through constant, intentional development.

The Role of Self-Assessment

The first step in designing a Personal Learning Plan is to conduct a self-assessment. It requires an honest and reflective assessment of your current skills, knowledge, and capabilities.

Ask yourself:

- What do I consistently do well?
- Where do I feel underprepared or less confident?
- What competencies are becoming more critical in my role or industry?

This process is akin to holding up a mirror to your professional self. It can feel uncomfortable, but it is essential. It helps you identify strengths to leverage, gaps to address, and priorities to focus on.

For example, consider an early-career project manager who excels at organizing tasks but feels less confident in communicating with stakeholders. Recognizing this gap is the first step toward closing it.

Setting SMART Learning Goals

Once you understand your needs, turn those insights into clear, actionable goals using the SMART framework:

- **Specific:** Define exactly what you want to learn.
- **Measurable:** Decide how you'll track progress.
- **Achievable:** Ensure your goal is realistic.

- **Relevant:** Align it with your role and aspirations.
- **Time-bound:** Set a clear deadline.

Instead of a vague intention like "improve leadership," a SMART goal might be "complete a leadership development course within the next three months and apply lessons in weekly team meetings."

SMART goals provide clarity, direction, and accountability (Doran, 1981).

Selecting Diverse Learning Resources

As discussed earlier in this chapter, it's essential to remember that an effective learning plan incorporates multiple learning modes. To highlight this again here:

- **Formal Learning:** Certifications, degrees, and structured courses that build credibility and depth.
- **Informal Learning:** Books, podcasts, webinars, and industry events that keep you current and engaged.
- **Experiential Learning:** Stretch assignments, cross-functional projects, volunteering, or mentoring others to turn knowledge into real-world practice.

Selecting resources is both strategic and personal. Consider your learning style:

- Do you thrive in structured, cohort-based courses with peer interaction?
- Or do you prefer self-paced, flexible learning you can fit around your schedule?

Building a Sustainable Learning Routine

Consistency is the key to the difference between good intentions and real progress. A Personal Learning Plan is most effective when it includes a realistic, sustainable routine.

Examples might include:

- **Daily:** 15 minutes of industry reading or language practice.
- **Weekly:** Completing course modules or journal reflections.
- **Monthly:** Progress reviews and goal adjustments.

A learning plan is not static. It should evolve with your goals and circumstances. Regular reflection ensures that your efforts remain aligned with what matters most (Brookfield, 2017).

Incorporating Mentorship and Feedback

Learning doesn't happen in isolation. Mentorship and feedback provide essential perspectives, guidance, and accountability.

- Seek out mentors within or beyond your organization who can share wisdom and help you navigate challenges.
- Participate in professional communities, forums, or networking groups to learn from peers.
- Establish regular check-ins to review progress, gain encouragement, and refine your approach.

Mentorship transforms learning from a solitary exercise into a collaborative journey. It offers real-world context, moral support, and sometimes even career-changing opportunities.

Example: Sam's Learning Journey

Consider Sam, a marketing associate aiming to move into a digital strategy role. While strong in creative content, Sam recognized through feedback and reflection that there were gaps in data analysis and strategic planning.

Sam used a Personal Learning Plan to turn this insight into action:

- **Self-Assessment:** Identified strengths in brand messaging and collaboration but acknowledged weaknesses in data analytics.
- **SMART Goals:** Committed to completing two certified courses in Google Analytics and strategy fundamentals within three months.
- **Resources:** Enrolled in online courses, read two industry books, and subscribed to a marketing podcast.
- **Routine:** Watched videos twice a week, completed assignments on weekends, and reviewed progress monthly.
- **Accountability:** Scheduled monthly mentor calls and joined a local marketing meetup group.

Sam's Personal Learning Plan Example

1. Self-Assessment

Strengths
Brand messaging, collaboration

Development Areas
Data analytics, strategic planning

What am i good at?
Where do I lack confidence

2. SMART Goals

Specific:
Complete twocertificed courses (Google Analytics, Strategy fundamentals)

Measurable: Two certificates earned

Achievable: Online courses with clear timelines

Relevant: For digital strategy role

Time-bound: 3 months

3. Learning Resources

Formal
Online courses (certifications)

Informal
2 industry books, marketing podcast

Experiential
Building a portfolio with data-informed strategy projects

4. Mentorship & Accountability

Mentor Calls
Monthly check-ins

Peer Learning
Local marketing meetup group

Feedback
Guidance, encouragement, real-worfu insights

4. Sustainable Routine

Weekly
Watch videos twice complete assignments on weekends

Monthly
Progress review, adjust goals

6. Reflection & Adaptation

Are goals still relevant?
Is the approach effective?
What's working or needs change?

Within 3 months. Sam completed both courses, built a strategy pos-tfolio, and confidently applied for

Within a quarter, Sam had completed the courses, built a data-informed strategy portfolio, and gained the confidence needed to interview for new roles.

Embracing Flexibility and Reflection

Finally, effective learning plans embrace adaptability. Not every resource will deliver as expected. Goals may need revising. Life may interrupt your routine.

Build in regular self-check-ins to ask:

- Are my goals still relevant?
- Is this approach effective?
- What's working well, and what isn't?

Regular self-check-ins ensure agility and intentional alignment with evolving professional visions (Senge, 2006).

Creating a Personal Learning Plan is the practical expression of lifelong learning. It takes you from theory to action, from curiosity to capability. By combining honest self-assessment, clear goals, diverse resources, sustainable routines, and supportive feedback, you turn learning from a vague ambition into a structured, lifelong habit.

This is how you not only stay prepared for the future of work but also actively shape it.

Section 3: Seeking and Using Feedback

In the journey of lifelong learning, knowledge alone is never enough. We can read books, attend workshops, and earn certifications, but without testing our assumptions or inviting input from others, our growth risks becoming one-sided and incomplete (Brookfield, 2017). Feedback is the critical mechanism that closes this gap.

Feedback acts as a mirror, revealing aspects of ourselves we can't see. It highlights strengths we can use with greater confidence, exposes blind spots that may limit our effectiveness, and clarifies expectations, aligning our actions with organizational needs (London & Smither, 2002). Far from being a threat, feedback is one of the most powerful accelerators of professional growth.

Yet feedback is often misunderstood, misused, or avoided. Many see it only in simplistic terms, praise to enjoy, criticism to endure, reducing it to a dreaded performance review instead of recognizing it as an ongoing resource for learning. In truth, meaningful feedback is a conversation that requires openness, humility, and a commitment to growth (Ashkanasy & Daus, 2005).

Embracing feedback requires a shift in mindset, moving from defensiveness to curiosity and from fearing judgment to welcoming guidance. Professionals who master this shift develop resilience and adaptability, become more self-aware, and build trusting, collaborative relationships that enable effective leadership (Stone & Heen, 2014).

This section will explore why feedback is indispensable to meaningful learning, highlighting how it transforms vague intentions into targeted development and keeps us grounded in real-world expectations. We'll examine the many forms feedback can take, from formal reviews to informal check-ins, peer conversations, and even self-reflection. You'll learn how to recognize and overcome common barriers to receiving feedback well and how to shift your mindset so feedback becomes a valued, natural part of your professional routine.

Most importantly, we'll examine practical strategies for consistently seeking, inviting, and applying feedback, making it an everyday habit rather than an occasional event. It includes integrating feedback into your workflow, improving your listening skills, and asking thoughtful questions that lead to valuable and actionable input.

By the end of this section, you'll see feedback not as something to fear but as an indispensable partner in your journey toward professional excellence. You will be equipped to seek it out with confidence, receive it with humility, and apply it with purpose, turning every conversation into an opportunity for learning, growth, and greater impact.

The Role of Feedback in Lifelong Learning

Feedback is the essential ingredient that transforms learning from a purely theoretical exercise into practical, meaningful growth (London & Smither, 2002). Without feedback, even our best efforts at self-improvement can remain unfocused or misguided. Feedback makes sure that our learning remains relevant and applicable, aligned with our real-world responsibilities, relationships, and goals.

Here's why feedback is so vital in lifelong learning:

- **It Reveals Blind Spots:** No matter how self-aware we try to be, we all have assumptions and habits we can't see. Feedback acts as a mirror that gently exposes these blind spots, allowing meaningful change before they limit our effectiveness (Senge, 2006).
- **It Clarifies Expectations:** We often assume we know what our team, clients, or industry expects, but those assumptions can be incomplete. Feedback aligns our efforts with what truly matters, removing guesswork (Ilgen et al., 1979).
- **It Reinforces Strengths:** Feedback is not just about identifying areas for improvement; it also reinforces the things we do well. Too often, professionals overlook their strengths, underutilizing the very skills that could set them apart. Constructive feedback shines a light on these assets, giving us the confidence and direction to use them more intentionally and effectively.
- **It Fuels Motivation and Engagement:** Even when feedback is challenging, it reflects that others care about our development. It validates our work and potential, providing direction and energy that self-guided learning alone can't (Ashkanasy & Daus, 2005).
- **It Encourages Adaptability:** In today's rapidly changing professional landscape, adaptability is not optional. Staying open to feedback means continuously learning, unlearning, and adjusting in response to new information or expectations. It develops our resilience and flexibility, ensuring we remain practical and relevant even as conditions evolve.

Professionals who actively seek out, listen to, and act on feedback distinguish themselves in any organization. They develop reputations for humility, openness, and a commitment to continuous improvement. These qualities foster trust among colleagues, strengthen relationships with clients, and position them as credible and reliable leaders.

In short, feedback is not just an add-on to learning; it is the vital process that grounds our development in reality and keeps us aligned with what truly matters. Embracing feedback transforms learning from an abstract goal into a powerful, ongoing practice of professional excellence.

Shifting Your Mindset About Feedback

Receiving feedback can feel uncomfortable, even threatening. For many professionals, feedback triggers anxiety about being judged, evaluated, or exposed. This is understandable: in traditional settings, feedback has often been treated as a formal, high-stakes event, similar to an annual performance review, where you're expected to either **"pass" or "fail."** This limited view turns feedback into something to endure rather than something to be welcomed and appreciated.

To truly grow and make the most of feedback, you must shift your perspective. Instead of seeing feedback as **criticism to fear or avoid**, you can choose to view it as a **tool**, a vital input that helps you learn more about yourself, your impact, and your development opportunities. This is the hallmark of professionals committed to continuous learning.

Shifting your mindset about feedback requires moving from **a defensive stance to one of curiosity**. It means recognizing that feedback is not about your worth as a person but about your potential as a professional. It's about being open to seeing what you cannot see on your own, blind spots, assumptions, and habits that limit you. It's also about surfacing and reinforcing your unique strengths so you can use them with greater confidence and impact.

When you choose to see feedback as a **continuous conversation rather than a one-time event**, you transform your relationships at work. Feedback becomes a regular part of collaboration, innovation, and leadership. It becomes a shared responsibility where everyone is invested in learning and improving together.

Feedback, at its best, is a **gift**, even when it's tough to hear. It gives clarity, offers perspective, and allows us to resolve minor issues before they turn into bigger problems. It demonstrates that others are invested in your success and trust you enough to be honest.

Ultimately, feedback is **a partnership**, not only with mentors and managers but with peers and even your direct reports. It's a collaborative process that supports everyone's growth, strengthens teams, and drives professional excellence.

In the following examples, you'll see how professionals have transformed their approach to feedback, from dreading it as criticism to embracing it as an essential resource for growth. These stories illustrate the powerful results that come when you choose curiosity over defensiveness and make feedback a natural, welcomed part of your learning journey.

1. Instead of Viewing Feedback as an Evaluation to Pass or Fail

Old Mindset:

"My performance review is a test. I need to prove I'm good enough and avoid criticism at all costs."

New Mindset:

"Feedback is data that helps me grow. It's a chance to understand what's working and where I can improve."

Merna, a mid-level manager, used to dread annual reviews, seeing them as scorecards that measured her worth. This anxiety led her to avoid tough conversations and gloss over areas needing improvement. After reframing her mindset, she began asking her manager during check-ins: "What's one thing I could do better this quarter?" This proactive approach turned intimidating reviews into a series of supportive coaching conversations that fueled steady, confident growth.

2. Instead of Seeing Feedback as a Threat to Your Self-Image

Old Mindset:

"If I get criticism, it means I'm not competent."

New Mindset:

"Feedback helps me see things I can't see myself. It's not about my worth, it's about my development."

Amro, a team lead, used to react defensively when colleagues offered suggestions, perceiving them as a challenge to his capabilities. After shifting his mindset, he practiced saying: "Thank you for sharing that. Can you help me understand it better?" This small change made others feel heard, encouraged open dialogue, and helped Daniel grow into a more respected and self-aware leader.

3. Instead of Responding Defensively, Choose Curiosity

Old Mindset:

"If someone gives me critical feedback, it means I'm not good at my job and I need to defend myself."

New Mindset:

"Feedback is valuable insight I can't get on my own. It helps me see blind spots, improve, and grow."

Ahmad, a senior director, used to feel attacked whenever colleagues offered suggestions, interpreting feedback as a threat to his competence. This led him to shut down discussions or argue his point, which created tension within his team. After reframing his mindset, Ahmad chose curiosity over defensiveness. He began asking questions like: "That's helpful, can you share more about what you noticed?" and "What would you do differently in my position?" These open responses signaled that he valued others' perspectives and genuinely wanted to learn. These qualities earned him greater trust and responsibility within the organization.

4. Seeing Feedback as a Continuous Conversation About Learning and Improvement

New Mindset:

"Feedback is most powerful when it's part of regular, shared dialogue."

Raj, a product manager, normalized feedback by weaving it into his team's weekly huddles. He asked: "What should we keep doing, stop doing, and start doing?" This simple practice transformed feedback into a routine, collaborative exercise that enhanced team communication and outcomes.

5. Viewing Feedback as a Partnership for Growth

New Mindset:

"Feedback is something we give and receive together to help everyone improve."

Jamal, a senior engineer, treated feedback as a shared responsibility. In team meetings, he'd say: "I want us to be comfortable giving each other feedback so we can all get better." By modeling openness and curiosity, he fostered a team culture where feedback flowed freely, thereby enhancing collaboration and performance.

This is the hallmark of the most successful professionals: they don't wait for change to force them to grow. They create systems, routines, and relationships that make continuous learning part of who they are (Brookfield, 2017). When you choose to embrace feedback and build learning plans around it, you don't just improve your skills; you shape your professional journey with purpose, resilience, and confidence.

Feedback is not criticism to be feared; it is insight to be valued. By seeking it out, listening with an open mind, and turning it into concrete learning plans, you make growth intentional and sustainable.

Advanced Techniques for Seeking and Applying Feedback

Feedback isn't just a single event or a yearly requirement; it's a continuous, strategic process that drives professional excellence.

While adopting a growth-oriented mindset is the foundation, truly effective professionals take it a step further: they build systems, habits, and conversations that make feedback an integral part of their daily work, learning, and leadership.

Figure 11 provides an overview of the three advanced techniques for seeking and applying feedback. Each is defined briefly and paired with practical steps for application. The following sections expand on these techniques in greater detail."

The following techniques offer practical, proven strategies with clear explanations and real-world examples, guiding you to consistently generate valuable feedback, transform it into actionable insights, and apply it effectively in your work.

Whether you're managing a team, collaborating with peers, or developing your skills, these approaches will help you make feedback a dependable driver of continuous improvement.

By adopting these methods, you can transform feedback from something you react to into something you actively harness, elevating your confidence, credibility, and professional impact.

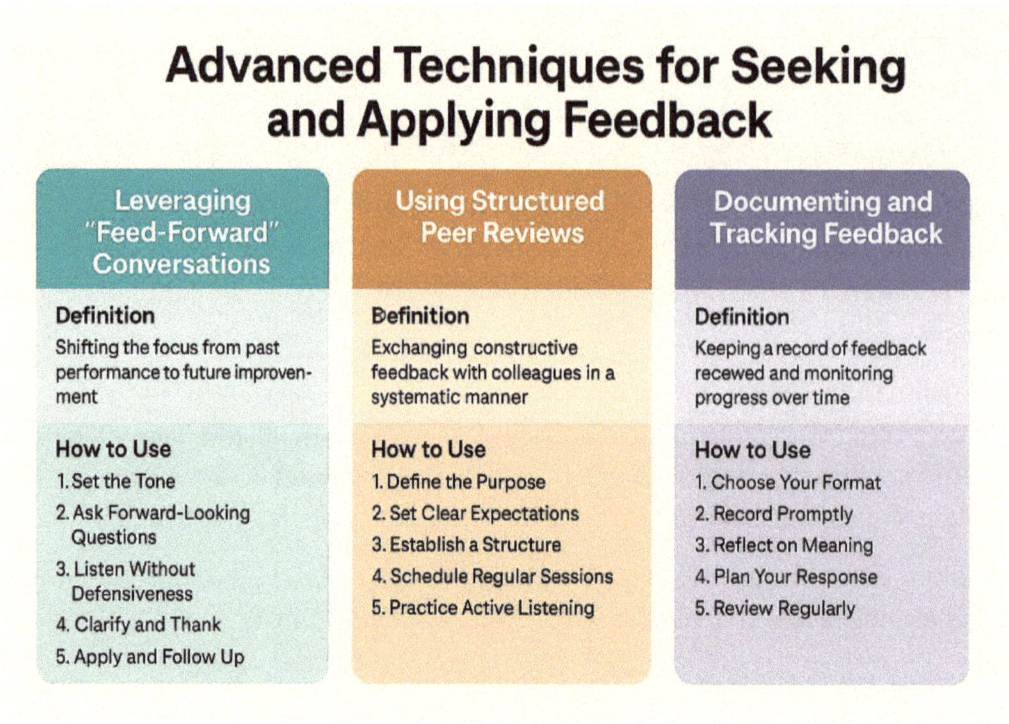

Advanced Techniques for Seeking and Applying Feedback

Leveraging "Feed-Forward" Conversations	Using Structured Peer Reviews	Documenting and Tracking Feedback
Definition Shifting the focus from past performance to future improvement	**Definition** Exchanging constructive feedback with colleagues in a systematic manner	**Definition** Keeping a record of feedback recewed and monitoring progress over time
How to Use 1. Set the Tone 2. Ask Forward-Looking Questions 3. Listen Without Defensiveness 4. Clarify and Thank 5. Apply and Follow Up	**How to Use** 1. Define the Purpose 2. Set Clear Expectations 3. Establish a Structure 4. Schedule Regular Sessions 5. Practice Active Listening	**How to Use** 1. Choose Your Format 2. Record Promptly 3. Reflect on Meaning 4. Plan Your Response 5. Review Regularly

Figure 11: Advanced Techniques for Applying Feedback

1. Leveraging "Feed-Forward" Conversations

Traditional feedback often focuses on dissecting what went wrong in the past, what you shouldn't have done, or what didn't work. While this can be useful, it can also trigger defensiveness, discomfort, or even shame. It can make people shut down instead of opening up.

Feed-forward is a simple but powerful shift in approach. Instead of asking "What did I do wrong?" you ask "What could I do better next time?" It turns the conversation from critical to constructive, from backward-looking blame to forward-focused solutions. This method encourages people to share insights, ideas, and suggestions without fear of blame or criticism (Goldsmith, 2003).

Why It Matters

- **Reduces Defensiveness**: By removing the emphasis on past mistakes, people feel less like they're being judged.
- **Promotes Collaboration**: It invites the other person to become a partner in your improvement, rather than an evaluator.
- **Generates Actionable Ideas**: The focus shifts from critique to practical, future-oriented advice.
- **Builds Trust and Rapport**: People see you as open, humble, and genuinely committed to growth.

How to Use This Technique

1. **Set the Tone:** Make it clear you want their input because you value their perspective.

2. **Ask Forward-Looking Questions:** Frame your question about the future, not the past.

- "What's one thing I could try to improve in our next project?"
- "How could I better support you in the future?"
- "What would you suggest I do differently next time?"

3. **Listen Without Defensiveness:** Don't argue or explain, listen.

4. **Clarify and Thank:** Ensure you understand, and express gratitude.

5. **Apply and Follow Up:** Implement the suggestion and check in later to demonstrate that you took it seriously.

Example in Practice

Sarah, a team supervisor, realized her weekly one-on-one check-ins had become uncomfortable for her team. She was focused on reviewing past errors, asking:

"Why didn't you hit your targets last quarter?"

This approach left her team members nervous and defensive. Realizing this wasn't working, she decided to shift to feed-forward questions. In her next round of meetings, she asked:

"What's one thing I could do differently next quarter to better support you and the team?"

The response was immediate and positive. Her team members suggested she could share priorities earlier in the week and hold a short Monday morning huddle to align everyone. Sarah implemented these ideas right away.

Within a few weeks, communication improved dramatically, morale rose, and her team began proactively offering ideas for improved workflows. Sarah's habit of asking forward-looking questions didn't just enhance her management; it transformed her team's culture into one of collaboration, openness, and collective problem-solving.

By embracing feed-forward conversations, you demonstrate your commitment to learning and growth, not only for yourself but also for your team. It's an approach that's easy to adopt, immediately reduces tension in feedback discussions, and consistently leads to more useful, actionable, and positive outcomes.

2. Using Structured Peer Reviews

In traditional feedback, the flow typically goes from managers to employees. But some of the most valuable, nuanced insights come from peers who work alongside you every day. Structured Peer Reviews create an intentional space for colleagues to exchange thoughtful, practical feedback about their work, fostering shared learning and collective improvement.

Why It Matters

- **Diverse Perspectives**: Peers see things managers might miss because they're directly involved in the work.
- **Uncovers Blind Spots**: Peer reviews reveal habits or choices you might not realize are barriers to success.
- **Builds Trust and Collaboration**: Giving and receiving feedback with peers creates a culture of openness and mutual respect.
- **Promotes Shared Learning**: Everyone benefits from seeing how others solve problems and approach tasks.

How to Use This Technique

1. **Define the Purpose:** Decide what you want feedback on, a project, report, presentation, or general work habits.

2. **Set Clear Expectations:** Agree that the goal is constructive improvement, not personal critique.

3. **Establish a Structure:** Use questions or frameworks to keep the conversation focused.

For example:

- "What's working well?"
- "What could be improved?"
- "Any suggestions for next time?"

4. **Schedule Regular Sessions:** Make peer reviews a normal, recurring part of your team's workflow, monthly, quarterly, or tied to project milestones.

5. **Practice Active Listening:** When receiving feedback, focus on understanding without defensiveness.

6. **Commit to Action:** Choose at least one piece of feedback to apply and revisit progress in the following review.

Example in Practice

An IT consulting team realized that while managers provided formal reviews, day-to-day collaboration wasn't generating enough meaningful feedback. To address this, they introduced monthly peer review sessions. Each consultant shared a recent deliverable, like a client report, technical design, or presentation, and invited colleagues to offer feedback using three questions:

- "What worked well?"
- "What could be clearer or more effective?"
- "Any ideas for next time?"

During one session, Elena, a new consultant, presented a client report. Her peers noted that while her analysis was strong, the language was dense and technical. They suggested simpler phrasing and clearer headings. Elena applied their feedback to her following report, which received glowing client reviews for its clarity and accessibility.

Over time, these peer reviews not only improved individual work quality but also strengthened team trust. Consultants felt more comfortable sharing challenges and seeking advice, creating a culture of continuous, collective learning.

By incorporating Structured Peer Reviews, teams move from isolated effort to shared growth. It's a practical, collaborative technique that makes feedback a regular, safe, and valuable part of professional development for everyone involved.

3. Documenting and Tracking Feedback

One of the most common mistakes professionals make with feedback is letting it disappear after the conversation ends. Even the most insightful feedback loses its power if it's not remembered, reviewed, and applied. Documenting and Tracking Feedback turns fleeting advice into an actionable learning resource you can revisit over time.

Why It Matters

- **Promotes Accountability**: Writing feedback down makes it harder to forget or ignore, helping you follow through on commitments.
- **Reveals Patterns:** Over time, you can spot recurring themes, both strengths to leverage and areas to improve.
- **Tracks Progress**: Reviewing past feedback shows how far you've come, reinforcing your growth mindset and motivating continued effort.
- **Improves Communication**: Sharing your progress with managers or mentors demonstrates professionalism and commitment to development.

How to Use This Technique

1. **Choose Your Format:** Use a notebook, a digital document, or a dedicated app, whatever makes it easy to maintain.

2. **Record Promptly:** After receiving feedback, note the key points while they're fresh. Include who gave it and in what context.

3. **Reflect on Meaning:** Ask yourself:

- "What's the core message here?"
- "How does this feedback connect to my goals?"

4. **Plan Your Response:** Outline clear, specific actions you'll take to apply the feedback.

5. Review Regularly: Schedule monthly or quarterly reviews to evaluate progress, update goals, and prepare for future conversations.

6. Share Selectively: When appropriate, share your progress with your manager or mentor to show your commitment to growth.

Example in Practice

Jonas, a senior analyst at a consulting firm, often received feedback in quick hallway chats or during busy project debriefs. He found himself forgetting important suggestions or failing to follow up consistently.

To address this, he started maintaining a "Feedback Tracker" in a simple notebook. After each feedback conversation, whether with his manager, peers, or clients, he'd jot down: key feedback points, why it mattered, and planned actions to address it.

For example, after his manager noted that his presentations were too data-heavy and lost the audience's attention, Jonas wrote:

Feedback: "Simplify slides. Focus on story, not just numbers."

Action Plan: "Revise slide decks with clear headlines and visuals. Practice storytelling approach."

Each month, Jonas reviewed his tracker, checking off improvements and identifying new goals. Over time, he noticed a clear evolution in his skills. He became known for compelling, clear presentations that resonated with clients.

During his annual review, Jonas shared highlights from his Feedback Tracker with his manager. He demonstrated not only his progress but also his disciplined, proactive approach to professional development.

By "Documenting and Tracking Feedback," you transform scattered, informal advice into a structured, personalized learning curriculum. It transforms feedback from something fleeting into a strategic, actionable plan for continuous growth, and proves to colleagues and leaders that you're serious about your professional development (London & Smither, 2002).

Feedback is a crucial pillar of professional growth, transforming abstract knowledge into meaningful, applied development. It serves as a mirror that reveals blind spots we can't see in ourselves, clarifies expectations, reinforces our strengths, and fuels motivation by showing that others are invested in our success.

When professionals treat feedback as an ongoing conversation rather than a one-time event, they cultivate openness, humility, and a commitment to continuous improvement. This approach strengthens relationships, builds trust, and positions them as credible, adaptable leaders. By consistently seeking, listening to, and applying feedback, we make growth intentional and sustainable, ensuring our learning remains connected to real-world needs and expectations.

Executive Snapshot – Chapter 3: Growth Orientation

Growth Orientation reframes work as an unending learning cycle. By adopting a growth mindset, building a personal development backlog, and transforming feedback into experiments, you accelerate skill acquisition and resilience. Successive small wins compound into exponential capability when tracked and celebrated deliberately. Let the recap steer your next sprint of continuous improvement.

- ✓ Adopt a growth mindset: interpret setbacks as data, not verdicts.
- ✓ Commit to continuous learning with a personal development backlog.
- ✓ Solicit feedback proactively and convert it into micro-experiments.
- ✓ Practice deliberate practice: repeat, measure, refine.
- ✓ Celebrate learning milestones, not just performance outcomes.
- ✓ Reframe failure stories to highlight lessons extracted and next steps.

Reflection Question: What single skill will you practise deliberately for 30 days, and how will you measure progress?

Chapter Four: Results-Driven Execution

In today's fast-paced professional landscape, where demands are constant, change is inevitable, and expectations keep growing, delivering real, measurable results is essential. Stakeholders, clients, and organizations aren't content with good ideas, detailed plans, or confident promises alone. They want outcomes they can see, measure, and trust.

Results-Driven Execution is the discipline of focusing your time, energy, and resources on what truly matters, ensuring that your work produces meaningful, sustained impact. It is the ability to translate strategic vision into consistent, high-quality delivery.

This chapter offers a practical, research-informed roadmap for mastering this vital pillar of professional excellence. It's structured into three integrated sections, each representing an essential building block of high-performance execution.

The first section, Rational Thinking – Clarifying and Planning, underscores that delivering results begins with disciplined, evidence-based analysis. Professionals who excel don't allow their efforts to be scattered across endless competing demands. Instead, they apply structured, critical thinking to identify what's most essential and chart the most effective course of action. It's about cutting through the noise to ensure you're tackling the right problems in the right way.

The second section, Accountability – Owning Results with Clarity, addresses the question: How do we ensure that our plans and priorities are realized? Rational thinking alone isn't enough without the structures, habits, and mindset that drive consistent execution. Accountability is the discipline that turns intentions into shared ownership, clear roles, and reliable follow-through. It's what transforms a plan on paper into action in the real world.

Finally, the third section, Outcomes – Delivering Reliably Under Pressure, focuses on the ultimate test of professionalism: producing meaningful results even when conditions are challenging. It's not enough to set goals or assign responsibilities; professionals must ensure those outcomes are consistently achieved, even as priorities shift and pressures mount. This final section addresses the real test of professionalism: producing consistent outcomes as priorities shift, pressures mount, and resources change.

Throughout this chapter, you'll find research-backed frameworks, practical tools, and real-world case studies designed to help you apply these principles in your own work. It's a comprehensive guide to help you become not only effective in your role but also a driver of excellence across your team and organization.

Results-driven execution isn't about striving for perfection. It's about practicing intentional, rational thinking, building disciplined accountability, and maintaining an unwavering focus on meaningful outcomes. Mastering these practices allows professionals to do more than stay busy. It enables them to deliver lasting value, which defines true professional excellence.

Section 1: Rational Thinking – Clarifying and Planning What Truly Matters

Rational Thinking is the cornerstone of professional excellence because it empowers individuals and teams to move beyond reactive habits and superficial fixes (Drucker, 1999; Kahneman, 2011). It demands that professionals slow down long enough to ask the right questions, define the real problems, weigh evidence over assumption, and design robust solutions that stand up to change. Rather than jumping to conclusions or relying solely on instinct, rational thinkers use structured analysis, creative exploration, intuitive judgment, and collaborative dialogue to make sense of complexity and chart a purposeful path forward (Mintzberg, 1994). This discipline directs time, energy, and resources toward what is most important, ensuring that work consistently achieves sustainable and high-impact results.

This section is designed to help you develop and strengthen this critical capability. You will explore strategic problem-solving, learning how to move from surface-level symptoms to root causes with structured tools and real-world frameworks. You'll discover how to define problems clearly, investigate them systematically, and generate solutions that are not only innovative but also feasible and aligned with organizational goals.

But solving the right problem is only part of the journey. You'll also learn the art of deliberate decision-making, a structured, intentional process that ensures choices are well-considered, transparent, and justifiable. You'll see how to clarify the decision context, generate and evaluate diverse options, make well-supported choices, and review outcomes to build institutional learning.

Next, we'll explore planning and forecasting, the essential disciplines that turn well-chosen solutions into real-world results. Effective professionals know that execution starts with design, not with action (Bossidy & Charan, 2002). You'll learn how to create actionable, aligned plans that anticipate risks, allocate resources wisely, and keep teams focused and coordinated.

Finally, you will dive into risk planning, the practice that transforms potential setbacks into manageable challenges. You'll learn how to systematically identify, assess, mitigate, and monitor risks, turning uncertainty into a source of competitive advantage rather than vulnerability.

Ultimately, this section is about elevating your professional discipline. It will challenge you to think with greater precision, design with greater foresight, and execute with greater confidence. By mastering rational thinking and its essential tools, problem-solving, decision-making, planning, forecasting, and risk management, you'll not only improve your own effectiveness but also strengthen your team's capacity to deliver consistent, high-quality results in an ever-changing environment.

Why Rational Thinking is Essential in Results-Driven Execution

In a world of constant demands and rising complexity, Rational Thinking is the discipline that helps professionals move beyond reactive habits and superficial fixes. It is the cornerstone of Results-Driven Execution, empowering individuals and teams to pause, ask the right questions, investigate root causes, weigh evidence over assumption, and design robust solutions that hold up under pressure and change (Kahneman, 2011; Mintzberg, 1994).

Rational Thinking is the foundation of effective execution. Without it:

- Teams waste time solving the wrong problems.
- Decisions are made on gut feel or habit instead of evidence.
- Plans fail to anticipate obstacles, leaving teams unprepared.
- Energy is scattered across low-impact activities.

With Rational Thinking, professionals transform uncertainty into clarity. They define exactly what problem they need to solve and why it matters. They weigh options thoughtfully, considering trade-offs and risks. They design action plans that are realistic, measurable, and aligned with strategic goals.

The Cognitive Palette: Thinking Styles

Highly effective professionals don't rely on a single mode of thought. They develop a flexible cognitive palette, adapting their thinking style to the demands of each situation (De Bono, 1999; Kahneman, 2011).

Each thinking style emphasizes a unique way of perceiving, processing, and responding to information. Understanding these distinctions enables individuals and teams to adapt flexibly to a wide range of challenges, ensuring that no problem is tackled with a one-size-fits-all approach.

Divergent thinking is the engine of idea generation. It emphasizes exploration, encouraging individuals to consider multiple, varied possibilities without judgment. This model is compelling during brainstorming or the early stages of innovation. A divergent thinker might ask, "What if we reversed the process entirely?" This opens the door to unconventional strategies. For example, when reimagining customer experience, a divergent approach invites options ranging from mobile-first journeys to gamified service models.

Creative thinking builds upon divergence by emphasizing originality and novelty. While divergent thinkers cast a wide net, creative thinkers focus on what stands out, ideas that challenge assumptions and spark innovation. Picture designers who eliminate text from meal kits, relying solely on icons and color codes to guide users, are inventive solutions that transform usability through simplicity.

Intuitive thinking draws from experience, instinct, and rapid pattern recognition. It proves especially valuable in high-pressure, time-sensitive environments like crisis response or medical triage, where exhaustive analysis isn't an option. Intuitive professionals make confident decisions based on subtle cues, even when formal data is incomplete or unavailable.

Convergent thinking operates as a filter, narrowing options to arrive at the most logical or practical solution. It's crucial in diagnostics, audits, and technical troubleshooting. Imagine an engineer dissecting system logs to trace the source of a malfunction. This thinking style excels in clarity, precision, and structured problem-solving.

Holistic thinking sees the forest, not just the trees. It takes into account the broader system, spotting interdependencies and anticipating ripple effects. In scenarios like organizational restructuring, a holistic thinker considers how altering reporting lines may impact culture, communication flow, and employee engagement, well beyond the org chart.

Rational thinking is grounded in evidence, logic, and analysis. It's the backbone of sound forecasting, strategic planning, and risk assessment. A finance professional modeling multiple economic scenarios to shape a five-year growth strategy exemplifies rational thinking at work, turning complex data into actionable decisions.

Collaborative thinking thrives in group dynamics, valuing collective intelligence and diverse viewpoints. In cross-functional teams, collaborative thinkers bridge the gaps between departments, ensuring alignment among marketing, operations, IT, and other areas. They foster co-creation, build consensus, and excel in environments where shared ownership drives success.

The following table provides a side-by-side comparison to reinforce these distinctions:

Style	What It Emphasizes	Hallmark Behaviors	When to Apply
Divergent	Breadth of ideas	Free-wheeling, "What if…?"	Brainstorming, early exploration
Creative	Novelty & originality	Seeks new patterns	Product design, strategy sessions
Intuitive	Feelings & hunches	Fast judgment, low data	Rapid triage, crisis response
Convergent	Single best answer	Evidence weighing	Root-cause analysis
Holistic	Whole-system view	Integrates parts	Change management
Rational	Verification by data	Tests assumptions	Forecasting, audits
Collaborative	Collective insight	Builds on others	Cross-functional teams

To deepen your awareness and sharpen your versatility as a thinker, take a moment to analyze your tendencies. Begin by identifying which of the seven styles you naturally gravitate toward in your day-to-day professional activities. Do you find comfort in structured, data-driven analysis (rational)? Or do you often jump to intuitive judgments based on your experience? Consider whether you spend enough time exploring imaginative possibilities (divergent/creative), or whether you rely heavily on group consensus (collaborative) without fully developing your own critical analysis.

Next, reflect on which style you may underutilize. For instance, if you're strong in convergent thinking but rarely practice divergent brainstorming, you might find yourself solving the wrong problem efficiently. Balance comes from the conscious application of multiple styles, not just proficiency in one.

As you navigate the following sections on problem-solving, decision-making, and planning, it is essential to recognize the value of intentionally applying diverse thinking styles. From divergent and convergent thinking to intuitive, rational, holistic, and collaborative approaches, each provides a unique way to explore challenges and opportunities. Leveraging these styles not only enhances the quality of insights but also expands the range of possible solutions. By aligning the proper thinking mode with the task at hand, professionals can approach problems more strategically, make decisions with greater clarity and confidence, and foster truly innovative outcomes. Practicing these thinking styles in a deliberate and integrated manner equips individuals to tackle complex situations with both structure and imagination.

Problem Solving – From Complexity to Clarity

In high-performing professional environments, problems are not interruptions; they are signals of growth, innovation, and unmet potential (Causevic & Lynch, 2019). Whether it's a decline in customer satisfaction, a recurring operational delay, or a gap in leadership development, the ability to confront and resolve problems strategically is a defining feature of professional excellence. Unlike reactive problem-solving, which is often driven by urgency, assumptions, or pressure to act, strategic problem-solving takes a measured and systematic approach. It begins with careful observation and inquiry, considers the broader context, and moves through a sequence of thoughtful stages that clarify not just what is happening, but *why* it is happening and *how* it can be resolved sustainably.

Too often, professionals are tempted to leap into solution mode. They identify surface-level symptoms and propose fixes based on past experiences or intuitive leaps. While these instincts may sometimes provide short-term relief, they often leave the deeper issue unresolved. Unlike reactive approaches, strategic problem-solving builds insight first to prevent wasted effort, misallocated resources, and unforeseen consequences. This approach does more than just fix what's broken. It equips individuals and organizations to solve the right problems at the right depth, creating not only resolution but also learning, alignment, and continuous improvement. At its best, strategic problem-solving turns into a culture, one where precision, transparency, and accountability are valued by all.

Professionals who embrace this discipline tend to demonstrate several hallmark traits:

- They ask better questions instead of jumping to conclusions.
- They engage stakeholders early to understand needs and pain points.
- They verify facts before developing solutions.
- They prioritize clarity over speed, recognizing that rushed fixes often require rework.
- And they document and reflect on outcomes to build institutional knowledge.

Strategic problem-solving is not a luxury; it is a core capability for navigating the complexity and ambiguity that define modern work (Bossidy & Charan, 2002). It transforms confusion into clarity, frustration into focus, and recurring problems into lasting solutions.

Structured Problem Solving: A Professional Framework in Action

Solving complex problems takes more than instinct or quick fixes; it requires a disciplined approach that combines critical thinking, structured tools, and strategic analysis. The following five-stage framework provides a systematic roadmap for addressing challenges, utilizing well-established techniques to ensure clarity, accuracy, and sustainable outcomes. Each stage is followed by a real-world example from TFS, a telecommunications company that successfully applied this model to address a significant performance issue.

Stage 1: Investigate the Context

Purpose:

Effective problem-solving begins with a deep understanding of the current situation. At this stage, professionals gather observable data, capture stakeholder perspectives, and identify patterns that may indicate broader systemic issues. Rather than rushing to conclusions, the goal is to build a complete picture of "what is" before asking "what should be."

Technique: Investigative Checklist

This structured approach includes the following guiding questions:

- Who is impacted?
- What is happening, and how frequently?
- Where and when is it occurring?
- What has changed recently?
- What do stakeholders say about it?

Applied Example – TFS Call Center:

TFS, a major telecommunications firm, experienced a 25% decline in call center sales over two quarters. Executives initially suspected poor agent scripting.

However, a senior manager initiated a comprehensive investigation:

- **Who is impacted?** Sales agents, dissatisfied customers, and overburdened team leaders.
- **What is happening?** Declining conversion rates, longer calls, and reduced upselling.
- **Where and when?** Issues were reported across East and Central hubs in all shifts, while the West hub remained unaffected.
- **What changed recently?** Onboarding was shortened from four weeks to two; as a result, employee turnover increased.
- **What do stakeholders say?** Agents felt unprepared, supervisors noted an increase in error correction, and customers complained about inconsistency.

This context revealed that the scripting concern was a symptom, not the root issue.

Stage 2: Define the Problem Clearly

Purpose:

A clearly defined problem statement aligns all stakeholders and ensures that attention is focused on solving the right issue. Without this clarity, teams risk spending resources on superficial symptoms rather than addressing core causes.

Technique: The 5Ws Problem Definition Formula

A precise problem statement answers:

- Who is affected?
- What is the deviation from expected performance?
- When did it begin, and how often does it occur?
- Where is it happening?
- Why does it matter?

Definition formula:

A problem is the gap between the current state and the desired state.

Applied Example – TFS Call Center:

Refined Problem Statement:

Since the onboarding program was shortened three months ago, TFS call centers in the East and Central regions have experienced a consistent 25% decline in sales conversions, longer call durations, and a decrease in upselling success. This has negatively affected agent confidence, customer satisfaction, and team leader capacity. This clear articulation served as a foundation for meaningful analysis.

Stage 3: Identify All Possible Causes

Purpose:

Jumping to conclusions can be a costly mistake. This stage requires divergent thinking to uncover every plausible cause across people, processes, tools, and environments. The goal is to explore possibilities without prematurely narrowing the field.

Techniques:

- **Cause-and-Effect Diagram (Fishbone/Ishikawa):**

The Cause-and-Effect Diagram, also known as the Fishbone Diagram or Ishikawa Diagram (Ishikawa, 1986), is a structured brainstorming tool for systematically identifying all potential causes of a problem.

Its purpose is to prevent teams from jumping to conclusions by organizing possible causes into logical categories such as People, Methods, Machines, Materials, Environment, and Measurements. This approach encourages divergent thinking, ensuring that no critical factor is overlooked, and helps teams visualize the complexity of contributing causes in a clear, easy-to-understand format.

- **Difference-Change Matrix:**

Its purpose is to systematically compare situations where a problem occurs versus where it does not, helping teams isolate variables that may be causal. By examining differences before and after the issue arises, or between affected and unaffected areas, professionals can identify specific changes that likely introduced the problem. This structured comparison reduces guesswork and speculation, leading to more focused, evidence-based hypotheses about root causes.

Applied Example – TFS Call Center:

The **Fishbone Diagram** for the TFS Call Center problem helps clarify why sales conversions declined by 25% after onboarding was shortened. The diagram organizes contributing factors into categories such as People (inadequate training, high turnover), Methods (compressed onboarding, weak coaching), Environment (competitive labor market, stress from targets), Technology (no system changes), Measurements (inconsistent tracking, lagging indicators), and Materials (outdated training scripts). By systematically exploring these categories, the team avoided blaming "poor scripting" alone and instead recognized that the issue was part of a broader, systemic challenge in workforce readiness and support.

This structured visualization enabled stakeholders to see the complexity of the problem clearly and ensured no critical factor was overlooked. It set the stage for further root cause analysis, such as using the *Difference-Change Matrix*, and guided the team toward targeted, sustainable solutions. Instead of reacting with superficial fixes, TFS could design a multi-pronged response, restoring onboarding duration, enhancing coaching, and improving retention, to address the real drivers of performance decline.

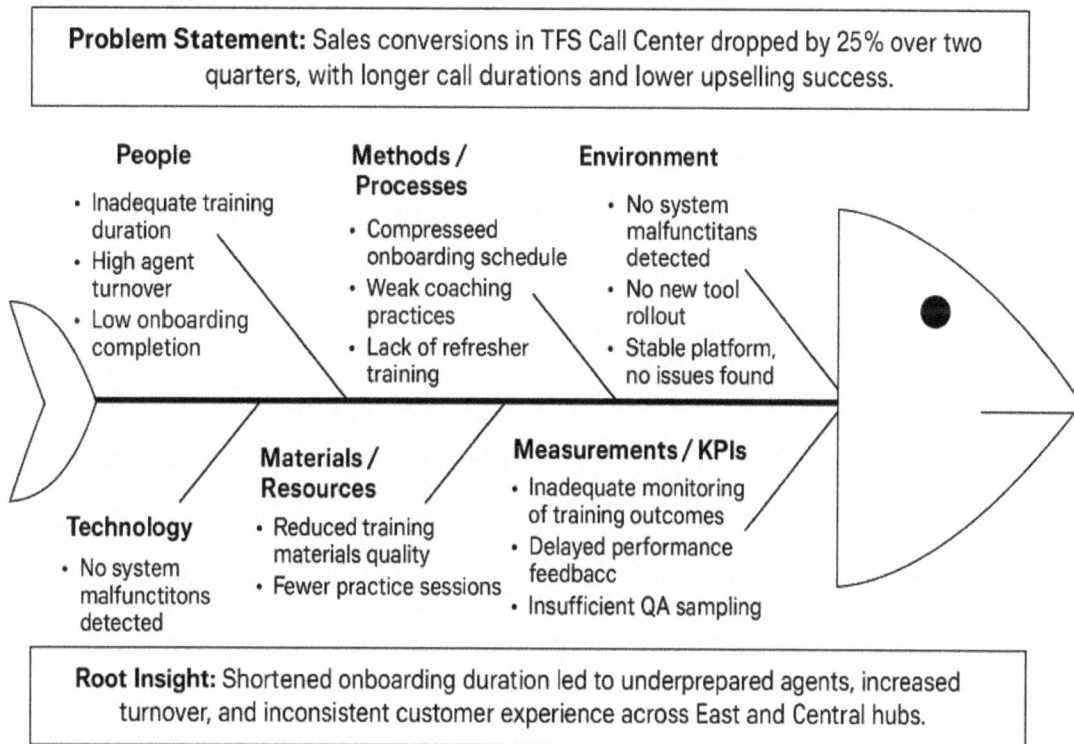

Problem Statement: Sales conversions in TFS Call Center dropped by 25% over two quarters, with longer call durations and lower upselling success.

People
- Inadequate training duration
- High agent turnover
- Low onboarding completion

Methods / Processes
- Compresseed onboarding schedule
- Weak coaching practices
- Lack of refresher training

Environment
- No system malfunctitans detected
- No new tool rollout
- Stable platform, no issues found

Technology
- No system malfunctitons detected

Materials / Resources
- Reduced training materials quality
- Fewer practice sessions

Measurements / KPIs
- Inadequate monitoring of training outcomes
- Delayed performance feedbacc
- Insufficient QA sampling

Root Insight: Shortened onboarding duration led to underprepared agents, increased turnover, and inconsistent customer experience across East and Central hubs.

Fishbone Diagram for TFS Call Center Performance Decline

The **Difference-Change Matrix** was used at TFS to systematically compare performance between the affected hubs (East and Central) and an unaffected hub (West), isolating variables contributing to a sharp decline in sales. The analysis revealed apparent differences: onboarding duration had been reduced to two weeks in the affected hubs, while it remained at four weeks in the West. This change coincided with higher agent turnover, a 25% drop in sales conversion rates, and increased call durations. Additionally, the frequency of upselling fell sharply where onboarding was cut, while supervisory workload increased due to more error corrections, and customer complaints rose because of inconsistent service.

This structured comparison reduced guesswork and speculation, enabling the team to move beyond surface-level scripting concerns and identify the actual underlying change that caused performance issues. By revealing how reduced onboarding and its ripple effects drove turnover and customer dissatisfaction, the matrix provided evidence-based insight that guided TFS toward meaningful interventions. Instead of addressing symptoms, the company can now focus its solutions on restoring onboarding duration, strengthening coaching, and managing turnover, tackling the root cause of declining sales performance.

Difference-Change Matrix: TFS Call Center Example

Factor	Affected Hubs (East, Central)	Unaffected Hub (West)	Difference / Change Identified
Onboarding Duration	Reduced to 2 weeks	Maintained at 4 weeks	Shorter onboarding in affected hubs
Agent Turnover	High	Low	Increased turnover linked to onboarding change
Sales Conversion Rate	Dropped by 25%	Stable	Conversion decline aligned with training cut
Call Duration	Increased by 12%	Stable	Longer calls in affected regions
Upselling Frequency	Decreased significantly	Stable	Drop in upselling success
Supervisory Workload	Increased error corrections	Normal	Higher workload due to undertrained agents
Customer Complaints	Increased inconsistency reports	Lower volume of complaints	More complaints about inconsistent experience

This broader analysis shifted focus from scripting to systemic workforce readiness and support challenges.

Stage 4: Confirm the Root Cause(s)

Purpose:

At this point, professionals must distinguish correlation from causation. The aim is to test assumptions and confirm which factors are truly driving the problem. Root causes are those that, if resolved, prevent the recurrence of the issue.

Technique: The Five Whys

This iterative questioning technique helps trace surface-level issues back to their deeper origin by asking "why" repeatedly until the fundamental cause is uncovered.

Applied Example – TFS Call Center:

- Why are conversions down? → Agents perform inconsistently.
- Why? → They're underprepared for calls and promotions.
- Why? → Training was shortened.
- Why was it shortened? → To reduce costs and respond to attrition.
- Why is attrition rising? → External market competition and limited development opportunities.

Confirmed Root Causes:

- Inadequate onboarding duration.
- Increased turnover without mitigation.
- Insufficient support from supervisors due to workload.

This diagnosis eliminated superficial fixes and targeted the real levers for performance improvement.

Stage 5: Generate and Prioritize Solutions

Purpose:

Once root causes have been validated, the final stage of problem-solving focuses on designing solutions that are both effective and practical. This phase requires *divergent thinking* to generate possible solutions creatively, and *convergent thinking* to systematically evaluate and prioritize them.

Technique: Solution Selection Matrix

A structured table helps evaluate each solution based on criteria such as impact, feasibility, cost, and implementation time.

Applied Example – TFS Call Center:

Solution	Impact	Feasibility	Cost	Time	Score
Restore Full Onboarding	High	Medium	Medium	2 months	17
Launch Retention Incentives	Medium	High	Medium	1 month	16
Introduce Peer Mentoring	Medium	High	Low	2 weeks	18

Final Actions

All three solutions were implemented in sequence. Peer mentoring was initially launched due to its ease and speed, followed by a restructured onboarding process and a tailored retention program.

In just 90 days, call center sales increased by 19%, agent satisfaction improved, and team leaders reported fewer performance issues, proving that the solutions tackled the problem at its core.

The TFS case highlights the importance of applying structured problem-solving in complex business environments. Each stage, context investigation, problem definition, root cause analysis, solution generation, and prioritization, plays a distinct role in achieving clarity and driving results. By combining analytical discipline with creative thinking and practical tools, professionals can move beyond surface fixes to implement lasting improvements.

Next, we turn to a discipline that is inseparable from effective problem-solving: decision-making. Diagnosing the right issues is only the beginning of professional excellence. Once we understand the true nature of the problem and its root causes, we face the critical question of what to do about it. Decision-making is the structured, intentional process of choosing among alternatives to achieve the best possible outcome.

Deliberate Decision Making – Choosing with Confidence

Every professional day is full of choices, some minor, some mission-critical. What makes one decision excellent and another regrettable often comes down to process. The best decision-makers strike a balance between instinct and evidence, speed and reflection, and autonomy and collaboration. They know when to pause and when to proceed (Hammond, Keeney, & Raiffa, 2015).

Unlike problem-solving, which seeks to understand and define what is going wrong, decision-making operates in a landscape where a problem or opportunity has already been identified. The goal is not to diagnose, but to decide: Which path forward creates the most value? Which trade-offs are acceptable? Which risks are worth managing?

High-quality decision-making is not just a technical exercise; it is a professional discipline. It blends rational analysis with stakeholder alignment, judgment, prioritization, and learning.

It requires clarity about what truly matters and the discipline to weigh facts over assumptions, as well as long-term impact over short-term comfort (Hammond et al., 2015).

Professionals who master this discipline cultivate a mindset of intentionality. They don't just make decisions, they architect them. They utilize structured processes to minimize cognitive bias, clearly define success, and ensure choices are made with precision rather than guesswork (Kahneman, 2011).

The Decision-Making Framework

The framework unfolds across five integrated steps, with tested tools, including decision matrices, impact assessments, stakeholder maps, and more, supporting each of these stages. What follows is an in-depth look at each phase of the framework, showing how professionals move from uncertainty to confident, informed action.

Step 1: Clarify the Decision Context

Purpose:
Before selecting a path forward, decision-makers must understand what they are trying to solve. This involves defining the objective, identifying boundaries (such as cost, time, and policies), understanding who is involved or impacted, and assessing the urgency of the decision. Without this clarity, teams may rush into decisions based on assumptions rather than facts.

Guiding Questions:

- What exactly are we deciding?
- What are we trying to achieve?
- What boundaries must we respect (budget, time, policies, values)?
- Who are the stakeholders?
- How urgent is the decision?

Example: HR Software Selection in a Large Organization

An organization recognizes that its existing HR system is outdated, leading to errors in payroll, fragmented employee records, and limited reporting capabilities. Early discussions revolved around "finding the most advanced HR platform." However, when the team clarified the decision context, they reframed the scope and focus of the decision:

- Objectives:

- Improve HR operational efficiency.
- Reduce payroll errors and manual data entry.
- Enable better employee self-service and reporting.

Constraints:

- Budget cap of $300,000.
- Implementation deadline of nine months to align with the new fiscal year.

- Compliance with labor regulations and data privacy policies.

- Stakeholders:

- HR leadership and staff.
- Payroll and Finance departments.
- IT team for integration.
- Employee representatives to ensure usability.

- Urgency:

- High, due to frequent payroll errors and employee complaints impacting morale and compliance risk.

Instead of asking "Which HR software is the most advanced on the market?", the team now frames the question more precisely: "Which HR solution can be implemented within our budget and timeline, integrates with existing systems, complies with regulations, and empowers HR and employees to work more efficiently?"

Step 2: Generate Viable Options

Purpose:
Professionals often fall into binary or "either/or" thinking, this vendor or that one, now or later. Effective decision makers go broader. Generating multiple, well-considered options fosters creativity, invites innovation, and uncovers potential trade-offs that otherwise remain hidden.

Techniques to Generate Options:

- Brainstorm with a cross-functional team.
- Challenge default assumptions (e.g., "What if we didn't switch systems?").
- Consider phased, hybrid, or unconventional solutions.
- Include external research or competitor benchmarking.

Example: HR Software Selection

The HR leadership, rather than limiting themselves to two known vendors, explores a full suite of possibilities:

1. **Vendor A:** Full-suite HRIS system with advanced AI and analytics.

2. **Vendor B:** Modular, cloud-based system with mobile capabilities.

3. **Upgrade Existing System:** Extend the system's life by two more years with add-ons.

4. **In-House Development:** Build a custom HR portal integrated with current tools.

5. **Outsource HR Operations:** Partner with a managed service provider for HR operations.

These five options represent a spectrum, from low-cost patches to bold, strategic shifts. Generating diverse options helps avoid tunnel vision and prepares the team for a well-rounded evaluation.

Step 3: Evaluate Options Using Clear Criteria

Purpose:

Once options are on the table, it's time to bring structure to the conversation. Without a shared evaluation framework, teams may default to relying on opinions or personal biases. This step introduces consistent, prioritized criteria so that each option is weighed fairly, transparently, and logically.

Tool: Weighted Decision Matrix

How it works:

1. List your criteria for success.
2. Assign a weight to each (based on importance).
3. Score each option (on a scale of 1–5 or 1–10).
4. Multiply score by weight and total up.

Example: HR Software Selection Evaluation

The team agrees on five criteria and weights:

Criteria	Weight
Integration with Payroll	30%
User Experience	25%
Time to Implement	20%
Cost	15%
Vendor Support & Reliability	10%

Options are then scored:

Criteria	Weight (%)	Vendor A	Vendor B	Upgrade	Custom Build	SaaS Model
Integration with Core Banking	30%	4	5	3	4	3
User Experience (UX)	25%	3	4	2	2	5
Time to Implement	20%	3	5	2	1	4
Compliance & Security	15%	5	4	4	5	3
Cost	10%	2	3	5	2	4
Total Score		350	440	290	285	380

Conclusion

- Vendor B emerges as the strongest candidate due to:
- Highest compatibility with existing banking infrastructure
- Fastest deployment timeline
- Excellent UX with moderate cost
- SaaS Model offers a strong alternative, particularly in terms of speed and user experience.
- Custom Build and Upgrade options score lower due to time, cost, and limited UX impact.

Step 4: Make the Decision

Purpose:

Now that the evaluation is complete, the decision must be made. This includes confirming alignment, reviewing assumptions, validating risk mitigation plans, and ensuring buy-in from all key stakeholders.

Checklist Before Final Decision:

- Are assumptions tested and validated?
- Have opposing viewpoints been discussed?
- Are we clear on both short- and long-term consequences?
- Is the decision documented and ready for communication?
- Who owns implementation and follow-up?

Example: HR Software Selection

The executive committee convenes with HR, Finance, and IT. After reviewing the evaluation matrix, the discussion initially favors Vendor A due to its features. However, Vendor B's faster deployment, modular pricing, and better usability prove more practical given the tight timeline and budget.

Final Decision:

Vendor B is selected. The implementation team is formed, timelines are shared, contracts are signed, and a communication plan is rolled out across the organization.

This decision is not just a choice; it becomes a coordinated action plan with roles, deadlines, and contingency planning.

Step 5: Review and Learn from Outcomes

Purpose:

Professional growth comes not only from good outcomes but from understanding how the decision-making process played out. Reviewing decisions, whether win or lose, builds institutional memory and enhances the quality of future choices.

Debrief Questions:

- What went well?
- What surprised us?
- Which assumptions held true? Which didn't?
- What would we do differently next time?
- How can we capture and share these learnings?

Example: HR Software Review – 6 Months Later

- **Successes:**
  - Payroll errors dropped by 70%.
  - 86% employee satisfaction with the new platform.
  - Training completed 2 weeks ahead of schedule.
- **Challenges:**
  - Integration with legacy systems required more custom work than expected.
  - A few remote offices had slower system access due to infrastructure gaps.

Lessons Logged in Decision Journal:

- Include IT's legacy system experts earlier in the evaluation.
- Add a "technical dependencies" criterion for future software choices.
- Allocate buffer time for training and change management.

The HR software selection example illustrates how structured decision-making transforms complex choices into clear, well-supported actions. By clarifying the decision context, generating diverse options, evaluating those options with transparent criteria, making the final selection with stakeholder alignment, and reviewing outcomes, professionals avoid impulsive, biased, or poorly considered choices. Instead, they ensure decisions are deliberate, evidence-based, and aligned with organizational goals. Every step in the decision-making process increases confidence, lowers risk, and fosters trust by ensuring the reasoning behind choices is transparent and justifiable. By combining analytical rigor with collaborative engagement, professionals elevate the quality of decisions and the impact of their execution.

Next, we turn to another critical discipline that builds on both problem-solving and decision-making: planning and forecasting. Once we have defined the right problem and chosen the best solution, we face the challenge of making that solution deliverable and predictable in the real world. Planning and forecasting are the professional practices that bridge vision and action. They ensure that goals are translated into clear milestones, resources are aligned, risks are anticipated, and teams know precisely what to do and when. This next section explores how professionals can design and execute tasks intentionally, avoid surprises, and consistently deliver results, even in dynamic and uncertain environments.

Planning and Forecasting – Designing Execution Before Acting

Delivering professional results begins not at the finish line, but at the drawing board. In high-performance environments, results are rarely the outcome of improvisation; they are the product of intentional design (Mintzberg, 1994; Meredith & Mantel, 2017). Planning and forecasting serve as the architectural blueprint for turning vision into a tangible impact. In a professional context, they are not merely operational necessities; they are foundational leadership disciplines.

Planning provides structure, sequence, and visibility. It empowers professionals to manage resources effectively, align teams, and translate abstract goals into practical workstreams. Forecasting, its strategic partner, offers foresight. It is a forward-looking process of anticipating events, variables, and conditions that could influence the execution journey (Makridakis et al., 2018). Together, they offer clarity before action and foresight before investment, empowering professionals to deliver not only on time, but on purpose.

Professionals who excel at planning and forecasting don't just hope for success; they design it. They move beyond vague intentions to actionable steps with clear milestones, well-assigned responsibilities, and built-in risk mitigation. This discipline ensures that once the right problem has been solved and the right decision made, execution is intentional, coordinated, and resilient to surprises.

Strategic and Operational Planning: Aligning Vision with Action

Professionals must navigate both the "big picture" and the "ground-level detail". This balance is achieved through two forms of planning:

- **Strategic Planning** defines long-term purpose and direction. It aligns teams with overarching institutional goals, identifies future priorities, and ensures that every action is connected to value creation.
- **Operational Planning** translates that strategy into day-to-day execution. It defines milestones, allocates resources, establishes accountability, and sets the rhythm for performance.

Example:

A regional bank outlines a five-year digital transformation strategy to shift 70% of its retail services to online platforms. This strategic plan sets key metrics: digital adoption, operational savings, and customer satisfaction targets. The operational plan for Year One then breaks this down into specific deliverables: redesigning the mobile interface, upgrading cybersecurity infrastructure, training service agents, and launching a campaign to encourage early adoption.

Without the seamless integration of both planning levels, execution becomes disjointed and reactive. But when aligned, strategic and operational plans function as the dual engines of intentional performance.

The Power of Forecasting: Seeing Before Acting

Forecasting is not guesswork; it is a disciplined form of anticipation. It uses data, trends, and historical insight to model likely outcomes (Makridakis et al., 2018). The objective is to minimize uncertainty and allow professionals to make informed, agile decisions.

Forecasting plays a central role in:

- Budgeting and resource allocation
- Demand estimation
- Project scheduling
- Market readiness assessments
- Staffing and recruitment planning

Example:

In a healthcare system, flu season forecasting utilizes epidemiological models, historical data, and current vaccination rates to predict patient volumes. This information informs resource planning, including staffing levels, supply chain orders, and contingency procedures. Similarly, in HR departments, attrition forecasting helps anticipate replacement hiring needs, prevent service gaps, and maintain productivity. By embedding forecasting into regular operations, professionals gain a proactive edge, spotting challenges before they become crises and identifying opportunities ahead of the competition.

Essential Tools for Structured Planning

Professionals don't succeed through vision alone; they rely on well-established planning tools to transform strategy into measurable, coordinated action (Meredith & Mantel, 2017). These tools provide clarity, reduce ambiguity, and ensure that every element of a plan is tracked, aligned, and risk-adjusted. Below are four essential tools, each with a distinct function and complementary value:

1. Gantt Charts: Visualizing Time and Tasks

Purpose:

A Gantt chart is a project management tool that provides a horizontal bar chart visualizing project tasks over time. Each bar represents a task, with its start and end dates mapped along a calendar timeline. Dependencies between tasks, what must be completed before another begins, can also be clearly displayed.

Professional Application:

- Clarifies the project timeline.
- Shows task durations and overlaps.
- Identifies who is responsible for what.
- Facilitates communication among stakeholders.

Standard Tools: Microsoft Project, Smartsheet, Monday.com, Excel (with templates)

2. Critical Path Method (CPM): Prioritizing the Timeline

Purpose:

The Critical Path Method identifies the most extended sequence of dependent tasks in a project, the "critical path," which determines the project's minimum completion time. Delays in any critical path task delay the entire project unless action is taken (Kerzner, 2017).

Professional Application:

- Determines project duration.
- Highlights tasks that must not slip.
- Allocates resources to critical activities.
- Enhances efficiency and accountability.

Steps to Apply CPM:

1. List all project activities.
2. Identify task dependencies and durations.
3. Develop a network diagram.
4. Identify the critical path (longest duration sequence).
5. Monitor and update as needed.

3. Scenario Planning: Preparing for Uncertainty

Purpose:

Scenario planning is a strategic tool that helps professionals prepare for multiple potential futures. Rather than relying on a single forecast, it creates structured narratives of best-case, worst-case, and most-likely scenarios (Schoemaker, 1995).

Professional Application:

- Enhances resilience in volatile environments.
- Improves long-term strategic thinking.
- Identifies decision thresholds and early warning indicators.
- Supports resource reallocation under different assumptions.

Steps to Apply:

1. Define driving forces (economic, social, technological).
2. Identify key uncertainties.
3. Construct multiple narrative futures.
4. Stress-test plans against each scenario.

4. Time Blocking: Structuring Personal Productivity

Purpose:

Time blocking assigns specific time slots to specific tasks or themes during the workday, preventing reactive scheduling and ensuring that deep, focused work receives adequate time and energy (Newport, 2016).

Professional Application:

- Prioritizes high-impact tasks.
- Minimizes distractions.
- Encourages proactive scheduling.
- Enhances time-awareness and discipline.

Steps to Apply:

1. Identify priority tasks for the week.
2. Estimate the time required for each.
3. Reserve blocks in your calendar (90–120 minutes max per deep work block).
4. Batch-related activities (e.g., emails, meetings).
5. Review and adapt weekly.

Case Study: Digital Banking Rollout – From Planning to Execution

Background:

A national bank launches a strategic initiative to roll out a new digital banking platform across 20 branches within six months. The goal is to modernize customer experience, improve transaction speed, and strengthen cybersecurity. The rollout includes infrastructure upgrades, platform development, regulatory compliance, training, and phased deployment.

To ensure disciplined execution, the project manager and team adopt four structured planning tools: Gantt Charts, Critical Path Method (CPM), Scenario Planning, and Time Blocking.

1. Gantt Chart: Structuring the Timeline

The team creates a Gantt Chart to visualize the entire project timeline. Each phase, such as requirement gathering, vendor selection, infrastructure setup, and user training, is mapped with clear start and end dates, showing dependencies and preventing overlaps.

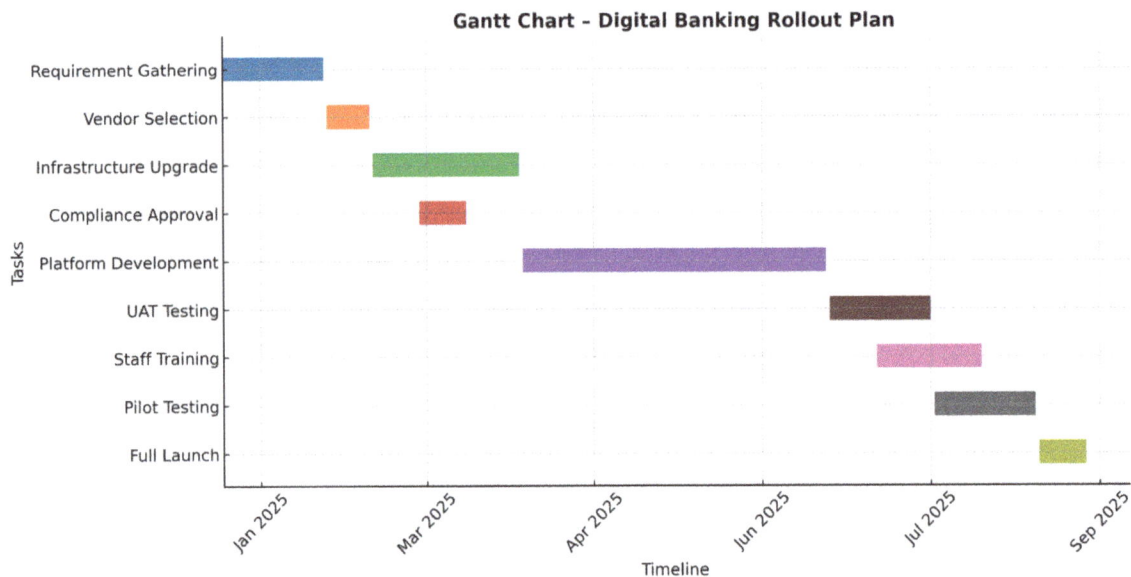

Gantt Chart - Digital Banking Rollout Plan

This visualization does more than schedule; it communicates. Stakeholders quickly grasp what happens when and which tasks run in parallel. For example, staff training and UAT testing are synchronized to save time, while vendor delays are monitored closely using milestone checkpoints.

Benefit: Enables clear tracking of progress and deadline management across departments.

2. CPM: Identifying Critical Priorities

Using the Critical Path Method (CPM), the project team identifies the chain of tasks that directly affect the project's completion time. Activities such as infrastructure upgrades, compliance approvals, and platform development are mapped with their respective durations and dependencies.

Digital Banking Rollout

Critical Path Method

——— Critical path

The CPM analysis reveals that any delays along this path will directly affect the final launch date. Consequently, these activities are given dedicated resources and risk buffers, while tasks outside the critical path (e.g., parallel staff onboarding) are given flexible timelines.

Benefit: Prioritizes resource allocation to the tasks that truly control project success.

3. Scenario Planning: Anticipating Uncertainty

Because the team anticipates variability in vendor reliability and regulatory review, they conduct a Scenario Planning exercise.

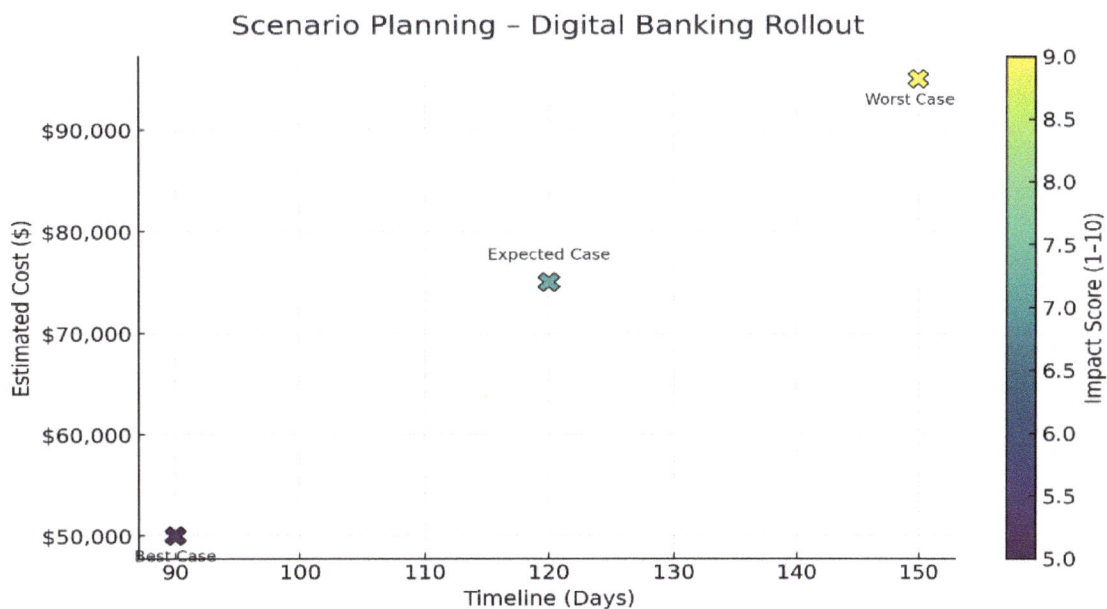

Three modeled scenarios emerge:

- Best Case: On-time vendor delivery and immediate regulatory approval → launch in 90 days at $50,000

- Expected Case: Moderate delays and one approval cycle → launch in 120 days at $75,000
- Worst Case: Two cycles of revision and vendor slippage → launch in 150 days at $100,000

This modeling helps the team build contingency plans, such as early document submission to regulators and establishing backup vendor support.

Benefit: Increases resilience by preparing the team for different possible futures.

4. Time Blocking: Daily Focus for Strategic Execution

The project manager uses Time Blocking to structure each workweek for strategic focus. Mornings are reserved for deep work, including data analysis, stakeholder planning, and platform review. Afternoons are reserved for collaborative meetings, compliance sessions, and scenario-building workshops.

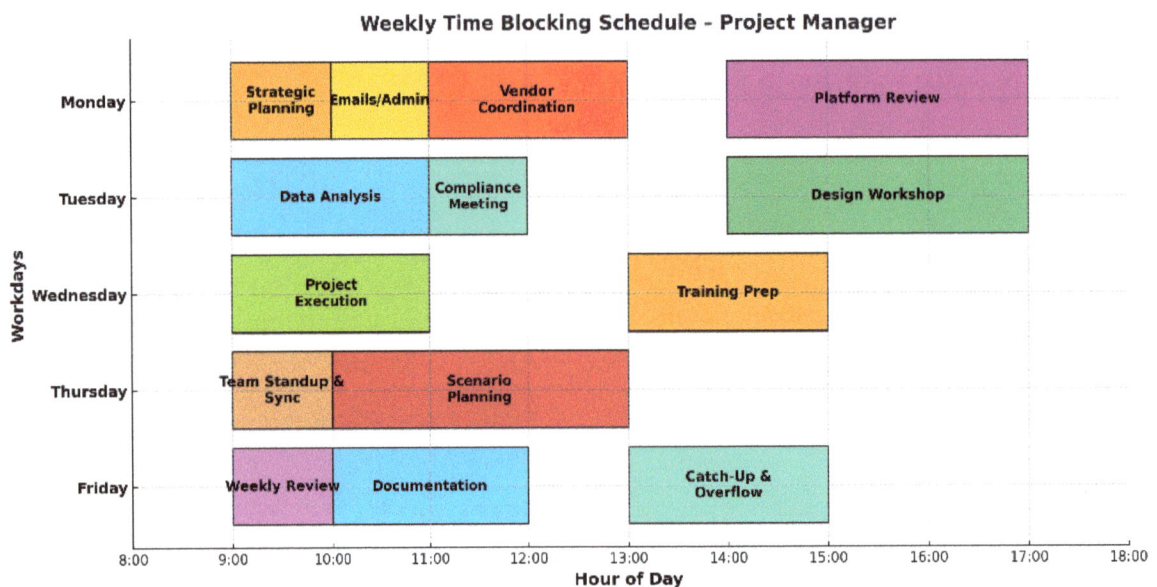

Weekly Time Blocking Schedule - Project Manager

Time blocking avoids constant firefighting. For instance, a two-hour daily block is allocated to "Issue Resolution & Vendor Communication," thereby reducing reactive disruptions throughout the day. Weekly review sessions track progress against the Gantt chart and adjust the time plan accordingly.

Benefit: Reinforces productivity by minimizing distractions and aligning execution with project milestones.

Integrated Outcome

Together, these four tools create a planning ecosystem:

- The Gantt Chart maps the timeline visually.
- CPM isolates the tasks with the highest strategic leverage.
- Scenario Planning prepares the team for variance.
- Time Blocking operationalizes execution at the individual level.

The result? The platform was launched two weeks ahead of schedule. Regulatory approvals go smoothly due to early submission. Training is streamlined, and technical issues are resolved proactively thanks to focused resource allocation.

This structured planning approach demonstrates how tools, when integrated rather than isolated, turn vision into execution and complexity into clarity.

Risk Planning: Thinking Beyond the Ideal

Even the most detailed plan is vulnerable to disruption. Risk planning prepares professionals to anticipate disruptions and respond decisively (Hillson, 2017).

Uncertainty is a given in high-stakes projects, not a surprise. Professionals who embed risk planning into their workflow convert vulnerability into foresight and chaos into control. They don't wait for problems; they anticipate, prepare, and create safeguards to protect progress.

Risk planning is a structured, proactive technique that identifies potential risks, estimates their severity and likelihood, and designs mitigation actions in advance. It fosters a culture of preparedness by minimizing surprises and facilitating faster recovery when issues arise.

This technique consists of four integrated steps that build upon one another:

1. **Identify Risks:** Generate a list of potential issues based on historical data, expert judgment, and context-specific analysis.
2. **Assess Probability and Impact:** Prioritize each risk using a numerical matrix to highlight where intervention is most urgent.
3. **Develop Mitigation Strategies:** Design safeguards or backup plans to reduce risk exposure or control the consequences.
4. **Monitor and Adapt:** Track the risk environment in real-time using dashboards and risk logs to stay agile throughout execution.

Let's walk through each step using a real-world example from the banking industry to demonstrate how risk planning elevates operational discipline.

Step 1: Identify the Risks

Risk identification is the foundation of risk planning. Professionals explore the full spectrum of what might go wrong, technically, operationally, financially, or reputationally. This is not a pessimistic exercise; it is a strategic inventory of potential vulnerabilities.

Case Context: Digital Banking Rollout

A regional bank is prepared to launch its new digital platform across 20 urban and rural branches. During the planning phase, the project steering committee conducted a cross-functional workshop to brainstorm risks. They generated the following list:

- App overload during peak hours
- Branch staff resistance to new technology
- Vendor's failure to deliver updated features on time
- Uncertainty over data compliance regulations
- Cyberattack through third-party APIs

Each of these risks had the potential to derail timelines, increase costs, or harm customer trust. Early identification gave the team a crucial head start in addressing them.

Step 2: Assess Probability and Impact

With risks identified, the next step is to quantify their severity using a **Risk Matrix**. This matrix evaluates each risk across two key dimensions:

- **Likelihood (L):** How likely is the risk to occur?
- **Impact (I):** How damaging would it be if it occurred?

Each is rated on a scale from 1 to 5, and the **Risk Score** is calculated as:

Risk Score = Likelihood × Impact

This numerical score (ranging from 1 to 25) allows the team to distinguish between critical risks that demand mitigation and lower-tier risks that require monitoring.

Banking Rollout Risk Matrix

Risk	Likelihood (1–5)	Impact (1–5)	Risk Score (L × I)
App Overload at Launch	4	5	20
Staff Resistance	3	4	12
Vendor Non-Performance	2	5	10
Regulatory Shifts	2	3	6
Cybersecurity Breach	5	5	25

High-risk items (≥16) are flagged for immediate mitigation. Medium risks (8–15) are tracked closely, and low risks (≤7) are noted for routine review.

Step 3: Develop Mitigation Strategies

Now the planning becomes proactive. For each risk, professionals ask:

- Can we **prevent** it from happening?
- If not, how can we **reduce** its probability or **limit** its impact?

Mitigation plans are documented, budgeted, and assigned to owners for execution.

Mitigation Actions for Digital Banking Rollout

Risk	Mitigation Strategy
App Overload	Implement a queuing system and cloud auto-scaling
Staff Resistance	Launch early training and appoint digital champions.
Vendor Non-Performance	Pre-vet secondary vendors and include penalty clauses.
Regulatory Shifts	Assign a legal team to monitor and pre-clear legal opinions.
Cybersecurity Breach	Conduct white-hat penetration tests and API code reviews

This stage transitions risk planning from a theoretical to a tactical approach. Each strategy is integrated into the project timeline and budget.

Step 4: Monitor and Adapt with a Risk Dashboard

Risk environments are dynamic. Even the best plans require continuous monitoring and real-time decision-making. For this purpose, the team uses a **Risk Dashboard**, a live visual tracker that consolidates key risks, mitigation progress, and status updates.

Here is the **Banking Rollout Risk Dashboard** used by the project steering committee:

Risk	Status	Owner	Next Action
App Overload	Red	IT Lead	Deploy a queuing system
Staff Resistance	Orange	HR Manager	Enhance peer coaching
Vendor Non-Performance	Orange	Procurement Officer	Confirm backup supplier
Regulatory Shifts	Green	Legal Advisor	Monitor for changes
Cybersecurity Breach	Red	Security Lead	Conduct a vulnerability scan

- **Red**: Immediate risk requiring urgent intervention
- **Orange**: Mitigation in progress or partial resolution
- **Green**: Low-risk, stable, or fully addressed

Weekly Risk Monitoring Dashboard

App Overload at Launch	IT Lead – Deploy queuing system
Staff Resistance	HR Manager – Enhance peer coaching
Vendor Non-Performance	Procurement Officer – Confirm backup supplier
Regulatory Shifts	Legal Advisor – Monitor for changes
Cybersecurity Breach	Security Lead – Conduct vulnerability scan

Weekly reviews of this dashboard keep the team agile and prevent last-minute crises.

Final Insight: Plan for the Real, Not Just the Ideal

Professionals don't only plan for what should happen; they also prepare for what might happen. That's the essence of risk planning: turning uncertainty into preparation and setbacks into manageable scenarios.

Whether you're rolling out a digital banking system, leading an HR transformation, or launching a new public service, robust risk planning equips your team to deliver with confidence, even in imperfect conditions.

Reflection: Elevating Your Planning Practice

Ask yourself:

- When was the last time you structured a plan that anticipated risk, forecasted trends, and aligned resources precisely?
- How do you currently prepare for unexpected changes? Are your fallback strategies reactive or embedded in your process?
- Do you use tools that help you visualize, sequence, and validate your assumptions?
- What could you improve in your next project by forecasting more deeply or planning more intentionally?

True professionalism is not just about delivering, it's about designing delivery with rigor, foresight, and purpose.

Section 2: Accountability – Owning Results with Clarity

In today's demanding professional environment, even the best strategies will fail without clear ownership and disciplined execution (Bossidy & Charan, 2002; Kotter, 2012). Rational thinking helps professionals define priorities and design solutions, but accountability ensures those plans deliver results (Drucker, 1999).

But accountability is often misunderstood. Accountability goes beyond blame and control. It's a mutual commitment to clearly define responsibilities, measure progress openly, and consistently honor obligations (Lencioni, 2002). It ensures that everyone knows their role, understands what success looks like, and can be relied on to do their part. In a culture of accountability, work becomes predictable, trust grows, and results align with strategy (Covey, 1989).

When accountability is absent, even the most talented teams can fail. Work is duplicated or neglected. Priorities are misaligned or forgotten. Communication breaks down, causing frustration, confusion, and wasted effort. Initiatives drift off course as busy professionals spend time on low-value tasks that don't truly move the needle. The result is eroded trust, squandered resources, and damaged credibility, not just for individuals, but for entire organizations (Kotter, 2012).

Accountability is not a one-time meeting or a checklist item; it is a culture built on shared expectations, clear roles, and visible progress (Bossidy & Charan, 2002). It transforms organizations by making sure that everyone delivers what they commit to, and that results, not effort alone, are the standard of success. In an accountability-driven culture, goals are specific and measurable, roles and responsibilities are clearly defined, and progress is tracked openly. Tools like dashboards and scorecards make performance visible, enabling constructive feedback and continuous improvement (Project Management Institute, 2017). Recognition focuses on meaningful outcomes rather than busyness, reinforcing a shared understanding that impact is what truly matters (Drucker, 1999).

Professionals who take accountability seriously don't just finish tasks; they make sure the right tasks are completed. They maintain clarity about what they are trying to achieve, follow through with discipline, and make their progress visible to others. They hold themselves and their teams responsible for delivering genuine value. As a result, they build trust with colleagues, leaders, and clients, enabling collaboration that multiplies individual effort into collective success (Covey, 1989).

This section explores how to build that culture of accountability in practice. It will show you how to create goal clarity, enforce disciplined execution, optimize resources, and track outcomes meaningfully. It will also demonstrate how to align roles through tools like the RACI Matrix, ensuring responsibilities are unambiguous and teamwork is seamless. By developing these habits and systems, you will not only deliver on your commitments but enable your entire team to work together with clarity, trust, and consistent impact.

Let's dive in and see how you can make accountability a defining strength of your professional practice, and of your organization's culture.

Results Orientation – From Activity to Impact

Results orientation is the mindset that separates professionals who work hard from those who truly deliver (Bossidy & Charan, 2002; Drucker, 1999). It is the habit of asking, "What outcomes am I accountable for?" rather than "What tasks did I do?" In many workplaces, there is a natural tendency to equate effort with value. Long hours, full calendars, endless meetings. But without clear goals and disciplined execution, busyness is just noise. Results orientation cuts through that noise. It is about defining success clearly and pursuing it relentlessly (Covey, 1989).

Four Essential Behaviors of Results Orientation

1. Goal Clarity

Professionals with a results orientation start by ensuring absolute clarity about what they are trying to achieve. They don't accept vague, generic objectives; they work to define specific, measurable outcomes that everyone understands and agrees on. This clarity aligns teams, guides prioritization, and lays the foundation for meaningful accountability (Drucker, 1999).

- Turn vague objectives into specific, measurable outcomes.
- Ask critical questions: What exactly are we trying to achieve? How will we know when we've succeeded?
- Align team understanding to prevent miscommunication or drift.

2. Execution Discipline

Clarity alone isn't enough without consistent, disciplined follow-through. Execution discipline is about maintaining focus on key goals even when faced with competing demands or obstacles (Bossidy & Charan, 2002). Professionals demonstrate discipline by managing their time intentionally, resisting distractions, and ensuring steady progress toward outcomes.

- Follow through consistently, even when priorities compete or challenges arise.
- Avoid distractions that dilute focus and effectiveness.
- Maintain momentum and reliability in pursuing goals.

3. Resource Awareness

Effective professionals are highly aware of the resources at their disposal and use them wisely. Resource awareness means optimizing time, people, and tools to deliver maximum impact while minimizing waste or unnecessary complexity (Project Management Institute, 2017). This ensures that teams operate efficiently and sustainably.

- Optimize the use of time, people, and tools.
- Prevent waste by streamlining processes.
- Avoid overcomplicating solutions that drain resources.

4. Outcome Tracking

Accurate results orientation requires not just setting goals but consistently measuring progress. Outcome tracking ensures that work is evaluated based on its real impact, rather than solely on activity (Kaplan & Norton, 1996). Professionals implement systems to make progress visible and encourage accountability at every stage.

- Measure progress in terms of actual results, not effort alone.
- Use dashboards, checklists, or reviews to keep goals visible.
- Enable timely adjustments and ensure accountability for delivery.

Professional Example:

Consider the case of a regional logistics manager who received a vague directive: "Improve delivery times." Rather than leaping into action without a clear target, she applied a disciplined, results-oriented approach:

- **Goal Clarity:** She redefined the objective with precision, setting a target of achieving 98% on-time deliveries within 60 days, making the goal specific, measurable, and time-bound.
- **Execution Discipline:** She implemented daily route audits and enforced weekly team reviews to ensure consistent progress and address obstacles proactively.
- **Resource Awareness:** She optimized existing resources by rescheduling loading windows to eliminate bottlenecks, achieving improvements without increasing headcount or adding overtime costs.
- **Outcome Tracking:** She introduced a live dashboard that displayed on-time performance by region and shift, keeping progress transparent and enabling quick corrective actions.

The team achieved the target two weeks ahead of schedule, all without additional costs, demonstrating the power of a disciplined, results-focused approach.

Role Clarity – Aligning Teams Through Clear Responsibilities

"Ambiguity is the enemy of accountability."

Even the most carefully defined goals and plans can fail if roles and responsibilities are not explicitly understood. Without clear ownership, work can easily be duplicated, neglected, or trapped in endless cycles of handoffs and approvals. When people are unsure of what they are responsible for, who has final authority, or when they should seek input, confusion replaces progress, and collaboration breaks down.

Role Clarity is the essential discipline that eliminates this confusion by making responsibilities explicit, visible, and shared.

This clarity promotes smooth collaboration and faster decision-making, freeing teams to focus on delivering real outcomes (Drucker, 1999). It ensures that every team member understands their specific role in achieving the overall goal.

116

When role clarity is in place:

- Everyone knows what they are directly responsible for.
- There is no doubt about who has ultimate accountability for delivering results.
- Those who need to be consulted are clearly identified, ensuring the right expertise and perspectives are included.
- Stakeholders who must be kept informed are defined in advance, promoting transparency and trust.
- By investing in role clarity, organizations create the conditions for smooth collaboration, faster decision-making, and aligned execution. Teams reduce friction and misunderstandings, freeing energy to focus on delivering real outcomes instead of managing internal confusion.

The RACI Matrix: A Tool for Clarity

One of the most effective and widely used tools for achieving role clarity is the RACI Matrix (Project Management Institute, 2017). This framework provides a straightforward yet effective way to define and communicate roles in any project or process, ensuring expectations are clear before work commences.

- **R – Responsible:** Who performs the task or work? This is the person or people who take action to complete the work.
- **A – Accountable:** Who ultimately owns the outcome? This is the person who ensures the work is completed satisfactorily and has final decision-making authority.
- **C – Consulted:** Who must be engaged for their input? These are subject matter experts or stakeholders who provide essential advice or perspectives.
- **I – Informed:** Who needs to be kept updated on progress? These are stakeholders who must be aware of decisions or outcomes, even if they aren't directly involved in doing the work.

By building a RACI Matrix during project planning or process design, teams clarify expectations up front. This prevents conflict later, reduces unnecessary back-and-forth, and ensures everyone knows their role in delivering success. It is especially valuable in cross-functional environments where responsibilities can become muddled or contested otherwise.

Professional Example

Consider a manufacturing plant that struggled with inconsistent quality reporting. Without clear role definitions, operators logged defects inconsistently, quality managers blamed production teams, and problem resolution stalled due to finger-pointing and confusion.

The plant's leadership implemented a **RACI Matrix** to bring clarity and alignment to the process:

- **Responsible:** Operators were clearly assigned the task of accurately logging all defects in real-time.
- **Accountable:** Quality managers took ownership of ensuring that defects were resolved and processes were improved.
- **Consulted:** Process engineers were engaged to analyze root causes and recommend changes to production methods.

117

- **Informed:** Supervisors were kept updated on trends, resolution rates, and improvement metrics to ensure oversight and drive accountability.

RACI Matrix for Quality Reporting in a Manufacturing Plant

Activity / Task	Operators	Quality Managers	Process Engineers	Supervisors
Log Defects	R			
Ensure Resolution		A		
Analyze Root Causes			C	
Track Trends & Progress				I

By explicitly defining these roles, the plant eliminated confusion and improved communication across teams. The result was a 22% reduction in defect rates within six months, along with a culture shift toward shared ownership and continuous improvement.

Building a Results-Focused Culture

Occasional inspections or one-time conversations cannot impose true accountability. To be effective and sustainable, it must be woven into the very culture of an organization. A results-driven culture is one where all employees, from the frontlines to senior leadership, are aligned in delivering meaningful outcomes, not just staying occupied.

In such a culture, results are not a personal choice or an individual standard; they are a collective norm. Expectations are clear, aligned, and consistently reinforced through structures, processes, and leadership behaviors. Teams understand not just what they need to do, but why it matters and how their work contributes to the organization's broader goals.

This shared understanding fosters trust, enhances collaboration, and ensures that accountability is seen not as control or punishment, but as a professional commitment to deliver value.

When accountability becomes cultural, it stops being dependent on individual discipline alone. Instead, the entire organization supports it through shared language, transparent systems, and consistent recognition. This makes accountability more resilient, even in times of rapid change, high pressure, or organizational growth.

Four Pillars of a Results-Focused Culture

1. Strategic Alignment via KPIs

For accountability to work at scale, daily work must align with organizational strategy. Strategic alignment means defining clear, meaningful **Key Performance Indicators (KPIs)** that cascade from top-level goals down to individual responsibilities. When everyone understands how their role directly contributes to success, they can prioritize the right work and see the purpose behind their efforts.

- Metrics must connect big-picture strategy to everyday tasks.
- Employees can see how their contributions drive organizational goals.
- Alignment prevents wasted effort on low-value or misaligned activities.

2. Recognition of Outcomes

Culture is shaped by what organizations celebrate. In a results-focused culture, recognition is reserved for real achievements that deliver value, rather than simply rewarding activity or effort for its own sake.

- Celebrating meaningful outcomes reinforces the expectation that impact matters.
- Teams learn to value effectiveness over busyness.
- Recognition becomes a tool for reinforcing desired behaviors and sustaining motivation.

3. Impact-Based Feedback

Feedback is an essential driver of professional growth and accountability. In a results-focused culture, feedback is grounded in actual outcomes rather than subjective impressions or effort alone.

- Reviews and coaching conversations focus on measurable results.
- Teams and individuals receive clear, constructive input about what is working and what needs adjustment.
- This approach encourages continuous learning and improvement while reducing ambiguity and frustration.

4. Tools and Transparency

Finally, accountability requires visibility. Transparent systems make progress and gaps clear to all, turning intentions into measurable commitments.

- Dashboards, scorecards, and project trackers ensure that performance is visible and shared.
- Teams can see progress toward goals in real time, enabling early problem-solving.
- Transparency builds trust by creating a shared understanding of expectations and results.

Case Study: Building a Results-Focused Culture at Apex Manufacturing

Background

Apex Manufacturing is a mid-sized, global producer of precision components for the automotive industry. Despite strong demand, the company was facing challenges with inconsistent product quality, missed delivery timelines, and declining employee morale. Leadership recognized that isolated training sessions and occasional audits weren't solving the real issue.

The problem wasn't about lacking technical competence or effort; it was the absence of accountability. Too often, teams worked hard but not always on the right priorities. Communication gaps led to finger-pointing, and initiatives lost momentum after initial enthusiasm. Leadership recognized that accountability needed to shift from individual discipline to an embedded cultural norm that was shared across the entire organization.

1. Strategic Alignment via KPIs

Challenge:

Employees complained that goals felt vague or disconnected from daily work. Production staff didn't see how their work impacted customer satisfaction or company profitability. Supervisors set targets inconsistently, and departments often worked at cross-purposes.

Approach:

Apex leadership started by clearly defining the company's strategic objectives, including reducing defect rates, improving on-time delivery, and boosting customer satisfaction scores. They then developed cascading KPIs:

- **Company-level:** Reduce defects by 25%, achieve 98% on-time delivery.
- **Department-level:** Quality team to achieve under 1% rework rate; Logistics to reduce late shipments by 4%.
- **Individual-level:** Machine operators to maintain daily defect rates under target thresholds; Shipping coordinators to hit 99% accuracy on orders.

Strategic Alignment KPI Dashboard

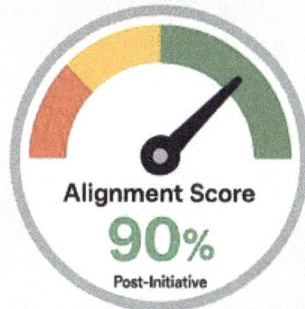

Alignment Score

90%

Post-Initiative

Company-Level KPIs

Defect Rate
↑ 25%

On-Time Delivery
98%

Department-Level KPIs

Quality Team
<1% Rework Rate

Logistics
4% Late Shipments

Individual-Level KPIs

Machine Operators
Daily defects consistently below threshold

Shipping Coordinators
99% Order Accuracy

Result

★ Improved role clarity

★ Increased motivation

★ Reduced misalignment

Strategic Alignment Dashboard

The "Strategic Alignment KPI Dashboard" visually communicates how Apex leadership addressed the challenge of vague, disconnected goals by cascading clear, measurable KPIs from the company level down to individual roles. At the top, the dashboard shows an impressive 90% alignment score achieved post-initiative, indicating strong cohesion across the organization. Company-level KPIs include a 25% reduction in defect rate and 98% on-time delivery, aligning with strategic objectives to boost customer satisfaction. Department-level KPIs focus the Quality Team on maintaining a <1% rework rate and Logistics on reducing late shipments to 4%. At the individual level, Machine Operators ensure defects remain consistently below target thresholds, while Shipping Coordinators maintain 99% order accuracy.

Together, this approach improves role clarity, increases motivation, and reduces misalignment, turning high-level strategy into daily operational discipline.

Managers were trained to hold monthly KPI alignment meetings, explaining why targets mattered and how individual roles contributed to success.

Employees reported feeling more explicit about expectations and more motivated, knowing exactly how their daily tasks connected to customer value and business performance. Misaligned efforts were reduced as teams shared a common purpose.

2. Recognition of Outcomes

Challenge:

Previously, recognition at Apex Manufacturing was informal and often based on perceived effort, long hours, or willingness to cover shifts, rather than actual results. This approach bred resentment, as top performers saw little difference in acknowledgment.

Approach:

Leadership redesigned recognition programs to celebrate real, measurable achievements.

- Monthly awards highlighted teams that met or exceeded KPIs.
- Success stories were shared in company newsletters and town halls, emphasizing concrete results such as improved quality metrics or delivery times.
- Leaders were trained to provide specific praise tied to outcomes (e.g., "Your team's reduced rework rate improved customer satisfaction scores this quarter.").

This shift reinforced the idea that impact, not busyness, was valued. Employees began focusing on delivering quality work rather than just being seen as busy. Motivation improved, with more staff volunteering ideas to hit and exceed targets.

3. Impact-Based Feedback

Challenge:

Performance reviews at Apex were infrequent, subjective, and often vague. Employees found feedback sessions unhelpful, describing them as "going through the motions" without any real learning or accountability.

Approach:

The company overhauled its feedback process to ground it in measurable results:

- Quarterly reviews now include KPI scorecards for every role.
- Managers were trained to prepare using data, highlighting specific successes and areas for improvement.
- Feedback discussions were reframed around outcomes: "How did your work impact defect rates or delivery times?"
- Employees were encouraged to reflect on their own performance and set outcome-focused goals for the next quarter.

Conversations became more constructive and actionable. Staff reported knowing exactly what was expected and what to improve. Trust in management grew as feedback was perceived as fair and objective.

4. Tools and Transparency

Challenge:

Apex lacked consistent systems to track and share progress. Data was often stored in spreadsheets or isolated reports, making it difficult for teams to see their performance in real-time.

Approach:

Apex invested in dashboards, scorecards, and visual management tools that made performance data transparent and accessible.

- Department-level dashboards showed live defect rates, delivery metrics, and safety incidents.
- Daily huddles reviewed these dashboards, enabling teams to spot and address problems early.
- Leadership used company-wide scorecards in monthly all-hands meetings to share progress toward strategic goals.

This visibility fostered a shared understanding and trust. Teams could see how their work contributed to company targets. Problems were identified quickly and solved collaboratively, reducing surprises and last-minute crises.

The "Apex Manufacturing Performance Dashboard" provides a clear snapshot of the company's operational performance, addressing earlier challenges where goals felt vague and disconnected from daily work. By defining and tracking key metrics, Apex leadership ensures everyone understands their role in delivering customer value. The dashboard reports a 1.5% defect rate, indicating strong quality control aligned with company-level goals to reduce defects. On-time delivery stands at 92%, showing reliable scheduling and logistics performance. Customer satisfaction is rated 4.6 out of 5, reflecting the impact of quality and service improvements on the customer experience. Meanwhile, two safety incidents are highlighted in red, signaling an area needing further attention. By visualizing these KPIs, Apex ensures consistent targets across departments, reinforces accountability, and supports continuous improvement toward strategic objectives.

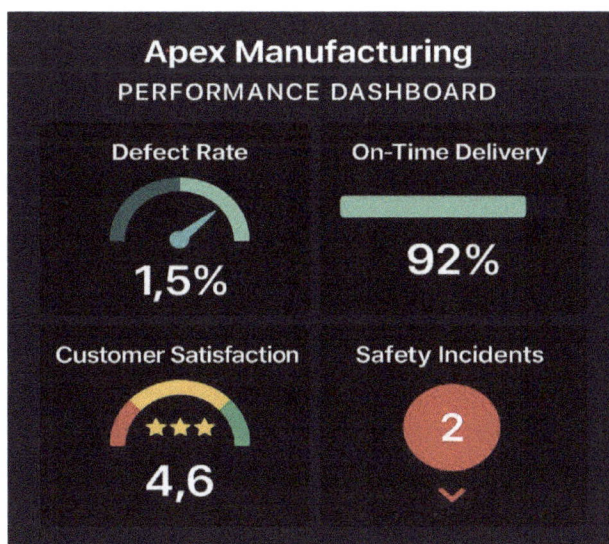

Apex Manufacturing Performance Dashboard Example

The "Apex Manufacturing Scorecard" provides a structured view of key operational metrics, comparing targets to actual results while offering status indicators and action-oriented comments. The Defect Rate is shown at 2.4%, meeting the target of under 2.5%, with a green checkmark and the comment "Achieved reduction in product defects." On-Time Delivery slightly misses its target of over 95%, coming in at 94%, flagged with a caution symbol and a note about "Implementing measures for improved reliability".

APEX MANUFACTURING SCORECARD

KPI	TARGET	ACTUAL	STATUS	COMMENTS
DEFECT RATE	< 2.5%	2.4%	✅	Achieved reduction in product defects
ON-TIME DELIVERY	> 95%	94%	⚠️	Implementing measures for improved reliability
CUSTOMER SATISFACTION	≥ 90%	92%	✅	Surpassed customer satisfaction goal
SAFETY INCIDENTS	≤ 5	7	❗	Additional safety training scheduled
KPI	TARGET	ACTUAL	STATUS	COMMENTS

Apex Manufacturing Scorecard Example

Customer Satisfaction exceeds its goal of ≥90% with an actual of 92%, earning a green checkmark and "Surpassed customer satisfaction goal." However, Safety Incidents is an area of concern: the actual value is seven, exceeding the target of ≤5, marked with a red warning icon, and the plan for "Additional safety training scheduled." Overall, this scorecard promotes accountability by clearly linking performance outcomes to management responses and improvement plans.

Overall Impact:

After one year of deliberately building a results-focused culture using these four pillars:

- Defect rates dropped by 28%, exceeding the target.
- On-time delivery improved from 85% to 97%.
- Customer satisfaction scores rose 20%, with clients specifically praising quality and reliability.
- Employee engagement surveys showed a 30% increase in staff feeling they understood expectations and their role in company success.
- Turnover declined, with exit interviews citing clearer expectations and fairer recognition as key improvements.

Building a results-focused culture is not about occasional inspections or top-down mandates. It requires intentional, consistent effort across strategy, recognition, feedback, and transparency. When accountability becomes everyone's shared expectation, organizations move from good intentions to sustained excellence.

Accountability turns plans into action and expectations into commitments. However, real professional excellence is demonstrated by consistently reliable results, even under pressure. The following section, Outcomes – Delivering Reliably Under Pressure, examines how to ensure that clear goals and accountable roles translate into measurable, sustained success in real-world conditions.

Section 3: Outcomes – Delivering Reliably Under Pressure

Even the clearest goals and the most detailed plans don't matter much if they fail to produce real, consistent results. Outcomes are the accurate measure of professional excellence; they're the evidence that ideas have been turned into meaningful, lasting impact (Drucker, 1999; Bossidy & Charan, 2002). In today's fast-paced, demanding, and unpredictable work environment, professionals must fulfill their promises despite shifting priorities, tight deadlines, limited resources, and unforeseen challenges (Heath & Heath, 2010). That's why disciplined, results-focused execution is so critical.

Outcomes don't just happen by chance or through good intentions alone. They are the result of deliberate, well-coordinated action that connects high-level strategy to the everyday work that gets things done (Rumelt, 2011). Professionals who excel under pressure know how to break ambitious goals down into specific, measurable achievements. They make sure every task and decision supports the larger mission. They understand that success isn't guaranteed by planning alone; it requires the discipline of steady follow-through, real-time problem-solving, and clear accountability (Bossidy & Charan, 2002; Duhigg, 2016).

This section is designed to help you master the practices that turn plans into results, not just once, but repeatedly and reliably as part of your day-to-day work. You'll learn how to close the stubborn gap between strategy and execution by turning big-picture goals into clear, actionable steps that guide what teams do every day.

You'll learn how to align goals with daily work, ensuring your organization's vision is not confined to strategy documents but is realized through concrete milestones, defined deliverables, and shared responsibility. This alignment makes strategy real, turning big ambitions into a series of achievable steps that everyone can own.

You'll explore structured prioritization, gaining the ability to tell the difference between what truly matters and what only seems urgent. Using practical tools like the Impact–Urgency Matrix, you can direct time and resources toward the work that delivers real value, helping you avoid the trap of being busy without being effective. This approach helps professionals work smarter, reduce wasted effort, and produce results even when demands are high.

Additionally, you'll explore how to make progress visible. By using tools like dashboards, milestone maps, and OKRs, you'll see how to make goals and progress clear and shared across your team. This visibility builds trust, supports problem-solving before issues become crises, and strengthens accountability, so everyone knows what's expected and how to keep work on track even when circumstances change.

Finally, this section will help you build the ability to deliver reliably under pressure. You'll learn how to stay focused, disciplined, and adaptable, even when you're facing tight deadlines, changing priorities, or unexpected obstacles. You'll learn how to prioritize in real-time, communicate openly with stakeholders, and proactively address risks before they become problems. This is the mark of professionals who can be counted on when it matters most.

Aligning Goals with Daily Work

One of the most persistent and costly challenges in organizations is the gap between strategy and execution. Leadership teams often invest substantial time and resources in developing ambitious strategies in annual planning cycles, strategic retreats, or leadership off-sites. They set inspiring visions, articulate bold priorities, and design targets intended to move the organization forward. Yet all too often, those strategies remain abstract and disconnected from the daily reality of When this disconnect exists, even dedicated teams can lose focus. They may be busy, but their efforts are fragmented or misaligned, resulting in inefficiencies, duplicated work, missed opportunities, and frustration. Without clear alignment, even the best-laid plans fail to deliver their promised impact (Rumelt, 2011).

Aligning goals with daily work is the discipline of making strategy real and actionable at every level of an organization. It requires deliberately translating high-level ambitions into clear, specific, and manageable actions that guide daily work. Professionals who excel at this understand that plans alone have no value if they can't be executed. They become bridges between vision and reality (Drucker, 1967).

Critically, this alignment is not about simply issuing top-down directives. It is a collaborative process in which leaders and teams work together to break strategic goals into operational milestones, define measurable targets, and assign clear responsibilities. This requires consistent communication of expectations so that everyone understands what they need to do, why it matters, and how success will be measured (Covey, 1989; McChesney, Covey, & Huling, 2012).

Alignment is also not a one-time exercise. Organizations function in dynamic environments where priorities change, obstacles arise, and new opportunities present themselves. Professionals need to regularly review progress, assess whether daily work remains aligned with strategic goals, and make necessary adjustments to stay on course (Kaplan & Norton, 2004).

Key Practices for Aligning Goals with Daily Work

1. **Break strategic goals into operational milestones.** High-level objectives should be decomposed into clear, sequential steps that teams can realistically deliver.
2. **Define daily or weekly deliverables.** Identify the specific actions and outputs required in the short term to advance milestones.
3. **Communicate expectations.** Ensure every team member understands their role, responsibilities, and how their work contributes to broader goals.
4. **Review and adjust regularly.** Schedule consistent check-ins to evaluate alignment, address obstacles, and refine plans as needed.

Consider a loan department in a regional bank that was struggling with long turnaround times and rising customer complaints. Leadership had set the strategic goal of "Improving customer responsiveness," but it remained vague until translated into specific, actionable work.

The department manager applied a disciplined approach aligned with the four key practices:

1. Break strategic goals into operational milestones:

The manager defined a concrete target: "Reduce loan application turnaround time by 17% within 90 days." This milestone provided a clear, time-bound objective to guide the planning process.

2. Define daily or weekly deliverables:

The team identified short-term actions to achieve this milestone, including daily reviews of loan processing queues, weekly progress audits on approval times, and scheduled training sessions to address knowledge or skill gaps.

3. Communicate expectations:

Roles and responsibilities were clearly outlined, so each team member knew their specific part in the plan. Staff were briefed on targets, individual and collective expectations, and how their daily work contributed to the department's broader goal of improving responsiveness.

4. Review and adjust regularly:

The team held structured weekly check-ins to assess progress against the target, identify new bottlenecks, and refine processes as needed. Adjustments included streamlining document verification and reallocating staff during peak periods to optimize efficiency.

By applying these four practices systematically, the department transformed a broad strategic ambition into concrete, daily actions. The result was that the team not only met but exceeded its turnaround time target ahead of schedule. Customer complaints declined significantly, and staff engagement improved thanks to shared clarity, ownership, and visible progress.

Prioritizing for Impact – The Impact–Urgency Matrix

One of the most common traps for professionals and teams is confusing busyness with effectiveness. In today's fast-paced, high-pressure work environments, it's all too easy to fill the day with meetings, messages, and low-value tasks while neglecting the work that truly drives meaningful results. Without deliberate prioritization, teams risk scattering their energy across too many activities and failing to deliver on the goals that matter most (Covey, 1989; McChesney et al., 2012).

Prioritizing for impact is the discipline of making conscious choices about where to focus time and resources to create maximum value. It's not about working harder, but about working smarter, choosing to do the right work at the right time. High-performing professionals and teams don't leave this to chance. They use structured, transparent methods to ensure that their efforts are directed where they'll have the most significant effect (Drucker, 1967).

A practical, proven tool for this is the Impact–Urgency Matrix. This framework helps teams evaluate tasks along two dimensions: how much they contribute to strategic goals (impact) and how quickly they demand attention (urgency). By plotting work against these dimensions, professionals can make more intentional and effective decisions about what to prioritize, defer, delegate, or eliminate.

This isn't just about managing time; it's about developing a strategic capability. It helps teams avoid the trap of reacting to every "urgent" demand at the expense of the truly important work that drives long-term success (Covey, 1989).

Key Practices for Prioritizing for Impact

1. **Identify tasks and evaluate impact.** Understand which activities most directly advance strategic goals or deliver meaningful value.
2. **Assess urgency honestly.** Determine when action is truly required, avoiding the trap of treating all demands as equally urgent.
3. **Classify using the matrix.** Place tasks into the four categories to guide decisions about scheduling, delegation, or elimination.
4. **Protect time for high-impact work.** Actively block and defend time for deep, strategic tasks that deliver the greatest value.

The Impact–Urgency Matrix Categories

- **High Impact, High Urgency:** Do it immediately. These tasks are mission-critical and time-sensitive.
- **High Impact, Low Urgency:** Schedule and protect time for deep work. These are the activities that create long-term value but can be overlooked if not planned.
- **Low Impact, High Urgency:** Delegate or manage carefully to avoid unnecessary disruption. These often distract from core goals.
- **Low Impact, Low Urgency:** Eliminate if possible. These tasks add little value and consume resources needlessly.

Consider a cross-functional team preparing for a significant product launch. Facing tight deadlines and an overwhelming list of tasks, the team applied the Impact–Urgency Matrix to prioritize effectively:

1. **Identify and evaluate:** The team began by listing all planned tasks and discussing how each contributed to the success of the launch.
2. **Assess urgency:** They determined which tasks had hard deadlines tied to the launch date versus those that could be done later.
3. **Classify using the matrix:**
    1. **High Impact, High Urgency:** Finalize customer onboarding materials, critical for launch readiness.
    2. **High Impact, Low Urgency:** Develop advanced training modules for post-launch support, which required deep focus but wasn't needed immediately.
    3. **Low Impact, High Urgency:** Respond to non-critical internal meeting requests that could be delegated to junior staff or rescheduled.
    4. **Low Impact, Low Urgency:** Review and archive old documentation, which was deferred entirely.

Impact-Urgency Matrix

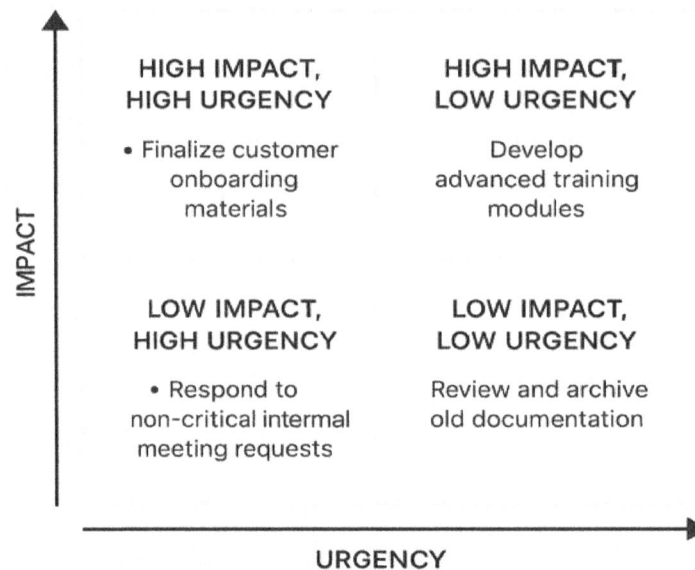

HIGH IMPACT, HIGH URGENCY		**HIGH IMPACT, LOW URGENCY**
• Finalize customer onboarding materials		Develop advanced training modules
LOW IMPACT, HIGH URGENCY		**LOW IMPACT, LOW URGENCY**
• Respond to non-critical internal meeting requests		Review and archive old documentation

Impact–Urgency Matrix for Product Launch Prioritization

5. **Protect time for high-impact work:** The team blocked dedicated work sessions for onboarding materials and scheduled focused time post-launch for training module development.

By rigorously applying this structured approach, the team ensured its energy was focused on work that directly supported a successful, on-time launch. They avoided last-minute crises, improved deliverable quality, and freed resources to address genuine priorities (McChesney et al., 2012).

When professionals consistently apply structured prioritization, they transform the way they work by ensuring that their energy is directed toward the highest-value activities. This disciplined approach not only enhances overall effectiveness but also minimizes wasted effort on low-impact tasks, improves decision-making under pressure, and guarantees that both time and resources are invested strategically in the work that truly advances organizational goals.

Making Performance Tangible – Visible Progress Tracking

One of the most powerful enablers of consistent, high-quality results is making progress visible. Too often, organizations set ambitious goals but fail to track them in a clear, shared, and actionable way. When progress remains locked in private spreadsheets, buried in disconnected updates, or left unspoken, accountability erodes, motivation weakens, and problems grow unnoticed until they escalate into crises (Bossidy & Charan, 2002).

Visible progress tracking is the practice of turning strategy from abstract intentions into operational reality. It's about making work transparent so that everyone understands where they are, where they're going, and what obstacles stand in the way. This shared visibility is not simply about oversight or control;

it is a form of empowerment. When professionals can see how their work contributes to broader goals, they gain clarity, purpose, and the confidence to make better decisions (Kaplan & Norton, 1996).

Visibility also supports proactive problem-solving. When teams have a clear view of their progress, they can identify issues early, make adjustments quickly, and collaborate more effectively. This reinforces a culture of accountability and continuous improvement, where success is measured not only by effort alone but also by real, meaningful outcomes.

Key Practices for Making Performance Tangible

1. **Define clear, measurable goals.** Establish precise targets that can be tracked objectively.
2. **Use consistent tracking tools.** Adopt systems and visuals that make progress easy to understand at a glance.
3. **Highlight both leading and lagging indicators.** Measure activities that drive success (leading) and the outcomes achieved (lagging).
4. **Share progress openly.** Make updates visible across teams to build trust, align expectations, and encourage collective ownership.

Essential Tools for Visible Tracking

- **Milestone Maps:** Timelines that break projects into clear checkpoints to track progress over time.
- **OKRs (Objectives and Key Results):** Frameworks that align individual and team goals with organizational strategy, ensuring focus and accountability (Doerr, 2018).
- **Daily/Weekly Trackers:** Tools that reinforce consistent behaviors and maintain momentum toward goals.

Consider a marketing team preparing to launch a national advertising campaign. Success depended on coordinated efforts across creative, analytics, and operations, with tight deadlines and ambitious engagement goals.

Applying these practices, the team:

- **Defined clear, measurable goals:** Targeting a 20% increase in engagement while maintaining budget discipline.
- **Implemented dashboards:** Tracked daily ad impressions, conversions, and spend in real time, enabling swift adjustments.
- **Used milestone maps:** Scheduled weekly checkpoints to review creative deliverables, approve assets, and assess campaign readiness.

The infographic titled "Used Milestone Maps" illustrates how scheduling weekly checkpoints improves project delivery and mitigates risks.

It features a clear timeline spanning four weeks, with labeled milestones for Creative Review in Week 1, Asset Approval in Week 2, and Readiness Assessment in Week 3. Simple icons visually reinforce each step, while the fourth week indicates continued tracking and preparation.

The lower section highlights the Results of this approach: improved on-time delivery of assets and avoidance of last-minute production bottlenecks.

The design emphasizes structured planning and proactive collaboration to keep marketing campaigns on track.

Used Milestone Map for Campaign Planning

- **Applied OKRs:** Aligned individual designer and analyst goals to the campaign's overarching target to ensure collective focus.

The infographic titled "OKRs Framework for Marketing Campaign Alignment" visually demonstrates how organizational strategy cascades into team and individual objectives to ensure focus and accountability.

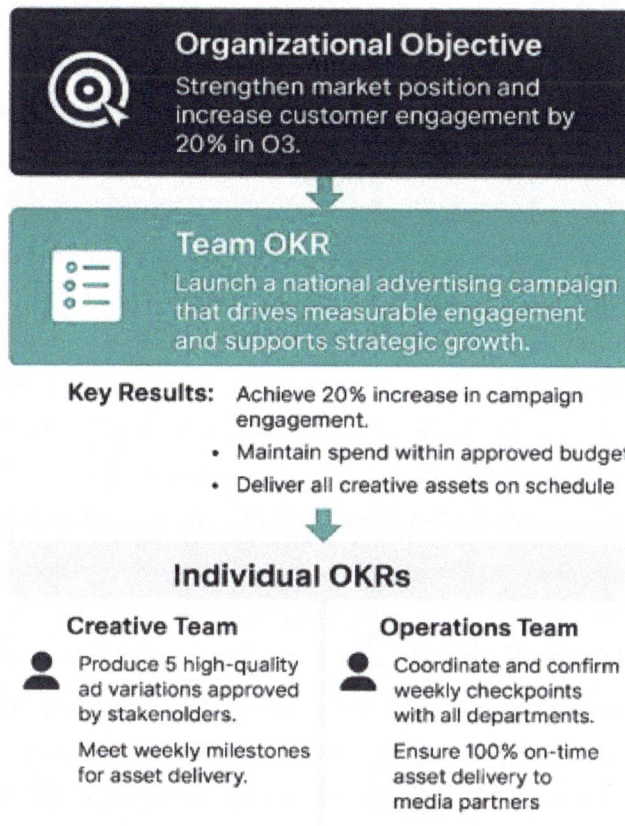

OKRs Framework for Marketing Campaign Alignment

Aligning individual, team, and organizinonal goals to drive focus and accountability

Organizational Objective
Strengthen market position and increase customer engagement by 20% in O3.

Team OKR
Launch a national advertising campaign that drives measurable engagement and supports strategic growth.

Key Results: Achieve 20% increase in campaign engagement.
- Maintain spend within approved budget.
- Deliver all creative assets on schedule

Individual OKRs

Creative Team
Produce 5 high-quality ad variations approved by stakenolders.

Meet weekly milestones for asset delivery.

Operations Team
Coordinate and confirm weekly checkpoints with all departments.

Ensure 100% on-time asset delivery to media partners

OKRs Framework

At the top level, it highlights the Organizational Objective of strengthening market position and increasing customer engagement by 20% in Q3. The Team OKR section details the marketing team's objective to launch a national advertising campaign with precise key results such as achieving 20% engagement growth, maintaining budget discipline, and delivering assets on time. The Individual OKRs section breaks this down further for specific roles, showcasing how the Creative Team commits to producing five approved ad variations on schedule. At the same time, the Operations Team coordinates weekly checkpoints and ensures 100% on-time delivery. Arrows visually connect each level, emphasizing alignment from strategy to execution.

As a result, the campaign not only met expectations but also exceeded engagement goals by 25% while staying under budget. The team attributed success to shared visibility, which kept everyone aligned, accountable, and focused on what mattered most.

When organizations embed visible progress tracking into their daily routines, they transform planning into action and intention into impact. Professionals can see where they stand, understand how to improve, and work together toward consistent, meaningful results.

Delivering Under Pressure

In a perfect world, projects would have generous timelines, unlimited resources, and steady, predictable conditions. The reality of modern professional life is far from ideal. Professionals regularly face tight deadlines, changing priorities, limited resources, and unforeseen crises, all of which test their ability to consistently deliver results (Heifetz & Linsky, 2002).

What separates exceptional professionals from the rest is not their ability to avoid pressure, but their capacity to deliver under it. This isn't about heroic last-minute saves or frantic multitasking. Instead, it requires clear thinking, disciplined execution, and proactive management to maintain quality and achieve goals even as circumstances change (Bossidy & Charan, 2002).

Delivering under pressure is the mark of true results-oriented professionalism. It reflects the ability to adapt strategically without losing sight of core objectives, to manage competing demands with intention, and to communicate transparently with stakeholders. Professionals who excel here earn a reputation for being dependable, effective, and capable of navigating complexity, a quality that is highly valued in any organization (Goleman, 1998).

Key Practices for Delivering Under Pressure

- **Real-Time Prioritization:** Adjust focus quickly in response to changing demands while keeping core goals at the forefront.
- **Selective Focus:** Say no to distractions and low-value work that doesn't meaningfully advance priorities.
- **Transparent Communication:** Keep stakeholders informed about progress, risks, and changes to manage expectations effectively.
- **Proactive Escalation:** Identify and raise critical issues early to secure needed support and prevent crises.

Consider an automotive manufacturing plant that suddenly faces a serious defect crisis, threatening its production schedule and customer commitments.

Applying these key practices, the plant's leadership team acted decisively:

- **Real-Time Prioritization:** Immediately reassessed production schedules, shifting resources to address the most urgent defect issues first.

- **Selective Focus:** Redirected teams away from non-critical tasks, concentrating all efforts on root-cause analysis and rapid resolution.
- **Transparent Communication:** Instituted daily updates for senior leadership and supplier partners to maintain alignment and manage expectations.
- **Proactive Escalation:** Escalated supplier quality problems to executive-level negotiations to secure prompt corrective action.

Through these disciplined steps, the plant reduced defect rates by over 30% in just eight weeks. The team not only overcame the crisis but also strengthened its processes for sustained quality and resilience in future challenges.

Delivering under pressure is not about frantic reactions; it's about a strategic response. It requires professionals to balance urgency with clarity, speed with quality, and responsiveness with intention. Teams that master this skill don't just navigate high-pressure situations; they build trust by proving they can be relied upon when it matters most.

Sustaining a Results-Focused Culture

Delivering results once is valuable, but true professional excellence is defined by consistent, repeatable success over time. One-off wins may create short-term impact, but organizations that excel do so by deliberately building and maintaining a culture that reinforces results-focused behaviors every day (Kotter, 2012).

A results-focused culture is not an accident. It doesn't depend on heroic individual efforts or bursts of last-minute energy. Instead, it is intentionally created through shared expectations, clear structures, and supportive systems that embed accountability and strategic alignment into daily work (Bossidy & Charan, 2002).

In such a culture, professionals are clear on what is expected, know how their work contributes to broader goals, and have the clarity to prioritize what matters, even in times of uncertainty or change. It is this clarity, combined with a commitment to continuous learning and adaptation, that ensures performance remains strong even as conditions change (Schein, 2010).

Key Practices for Sustaining a Results-Focused Culture:

- **Alignment:** Connect goals, roles, and metrics so that everyone understands how their work contributes to strategic priorities. Alignment ensures that efforts are not fragmented or misdirected.
- **Ownership:** Make accountability explicit. Everyone knows what they are responsible for delivering, and commits to following through. This clarity prevents gaps, overlaps, and confusion about expectations.
- **Recognition:** Celebrate and reward meaningful outcomes, reinforcing the behaviors that deliver real value. Recognition builds morale, motivation, and reinforces what the organization values most.

- **Adaptation:** Foster continuous learning by encouraging teams to reflect on successes and challenges, share insights, and improve processes over time. This ensures the culture evolves and remains effective as circumstances change.

Consider a technology firm that struggled with missed project deadlines, resulting in client dissatisfaction and lost revenue. Leadership recognized that sporadic focus and unclear accountability were hindering their progress.

They took deliberate steps to build a results-focused culture:

- **Alignment:** Introduced OKRs (Objectives and Key Results) across departments, ensuring every team and individual goal directly supported company priorities.
- **Ownership:** Clarified individual responsibilities for critical project tasks, making sure no work fell through the cracks.
- **Recognition:** Celebrated successful launches publicly, highlighting teams that met or exceeded targets to reinforce desired behaviors.
- **Adaptation:** Conducted structured retrospectives after each project, identifying lessons learned and embedding improvements into future planning.

These changes transformed the firm's approach. On-time delivery rates improved dramatically, from 60% to over 90% in a single year. More importantly, the organization built a sustainable system where high performance became the norm, not the exception.

Sustaining a results-focused culture is not about rigid control or micromanagement. It's about creating an environment where professionals have the clarity, support, and shared understanding necessary to deliver consistent, meaningful outcomes. When goals are aligned, accountability is clear, recognition is meaningful, and learning is continuous, organizations can maintain high performance even as they grow or adapt to new challenges (Kotter, 2012; Schein, 2010).

This integration turns good intentions into sustained results. It ensures that clear goals, aligned roles, and shared accountability are not just aspirational values but everyday operational realities. Teams develop the discipline to prioritize what matters most, adapt proactively to new challenges, and maintain focus and quality even under pressure.

In doing so, organizations build lasting trust with customers, stakeholders, and employees alike, establishing a reputation for excellence that endures regardless of circumstances.

Executive Snapshot – Chapter 4: Results-Driven Execution

In Results-Driven Execution, you transformed strategy into action. You practised setting measurable objectives, prioritising tasks by impact, and keeping momentum through rigorous review cycles. Execution excellence is a discipline: choose fewer goals, measure them relentlessly, and course-correct before drift becomes failure. The box below crystallises the execution habits that keep progress visible and accountable.

✓ Translate strategy into measurable objectives (OKRs/KPIs) with clear owners.
✓ Prioritise ruthlessly: focus on high-impact tasks (Pareto 80/20).
✓ Forecast and plan using rolling horizons to stay ahead of risk.
✓ Apply accountability frameworks (RACI, scorecards) to keep momentum.
✓ Track leading indicators weekly; adjust tactics early.
✓ Celebrate wins and codify lessons learned in a 'playbook'.

Reflection Question: Which single KPI will you review weekly to stay laser-focused on outcomes?

Chapter Five: Strategic Connection

Strategic Connection is one of the essential pillars of professional excellence because in today's highly interconnected, fast-moving world, no one achieves meaningful, sustainable success alone. It's easy to think that talent and ambition can carry someone forward, but the reality is different. The challenges professionals face are layered and demanding, and the pace of change makes it impossible to succeed in isolation.

This chapter offers a practical, research-informed roadmap for mastering Strategic Connection, organized into three integrated sections.

The first section, "Networking – Expanding Your Professional Reach," focuses on building a purposeful and strategic network that delivers lasting value throughout your career. Too often, networking is misunderstood as shallow socializing or self-serving promotion. In truth, effective networking is about cultivating genuine, diverse, and mutually beneficial relationships. You'll learn how to identify key stakeholders, map your network strategically, and engage meaningfully with people across roles, functions, and industries to create opportunities and expand your perspective.

The second section, "Collaboration – Achieving More Together," explores how to transform those connections into productive partnerships that deliver results. Networking lays the foundation by creating connections; collaboration is what turns them into shared success. This section examines the mindset and skills needed to work effectively with others toward common goals. You'll learn how to bring clarity to shared objectives, establish clear responsibilities, and keep communication open. Along the way, you'll gain strategies to handle conflict in a constructive way while balancing different perspectives so trust grows and the team stays focused on its goals.

The third section, "Value Exchange – Building Trust and Mutual Benefit," dives into the core of every enduring professional relationship: trust and reciprocity. This section explains how to understand and align with others' interests, communicate your value clearly and authentically, and reliably deliver on your commitments. You'll explore practical frameworks for maintaining trust even when things get tough, creating win–win scenarios in negotiations, and reinforcing your professional integrity in every interaction.

Together, these three sections form a comprehensive approach to Strategic Connection. Networking expands your reach and gives you access to new opportunities and ideas. Collaboration turns that network into productive, goal-focused partnerships. Value Exchange ensures those relationships remain strong, authentic, and mutually beneficial over time.

Section 1: Networking – Expanding Your Professional Reach

Networking is the first essential dimension of Strategic Connection. It is the proactive, intentional process of building and maintaining relationships that extend your reach, influence, and opportunities. Effective networking goes well beyond swapping business cards or adding contacts online. It's about creating genuine, reciprocal relationships that not only support your own goals but also contribute to the success of others over time (Ibarra & Hunter, 2007; Uzzi & Dunlap, 2005).

Networking adds significant value to your professional journey by opening access to resources, insights, collaborations, and opportunities that would be unreachable in isolation. It is not just a social exercise but a strategic asset that can accelerate problem-solving, career growth, innovation, and organizational impact (Cross et al., 2016). By cultivating trust-based relationships across functions, industries, and cultures, professionals can anticipate trends, respond more effectively to challenges, and gain fresh perspectives that improve decision-making and performance (Burt, 2004; Granovetter, 1983).

Importantly, networking should not be seen as something reserved only for job searches or sales opportunities. It is a continuous professional discipline that should be integrated into all stages of your career. When entering a new role or organization, networking helps you learn the landscape, identify key influencers, and establish early rapport. When leading projects, it enables you to secure buy-in, access resources, and manage stakeholders effectively. During times of change or uncertainty, networking becomes crucial for gathering diverse perspectives and staying informed about emerging trends. For career development, it unlocks mentorship, helps you explore new paths, and maintains your visibility in your field. When tackling complex problems, it provides access to collective expertise and reveals innovative solutions (Higgins & Kram, 2001).

Implementing networking professionally and effectively requires a giving mindset. It should be approached as a two-way exchange in which you offer help, share information, and create value for others without expecting immediate returns (Blau, 1964; Covey, 2006). It also requires a clear sense of purpose. You need to know what you want to achieve through your network, whether that is guidance, opportunities to collaborate, or progress in your career, and then focus on building the kinds of connections that genuinely support those aims. Prioritizing quality over quantity is essential: meaningful, authentic relationships matter far more than superficial contacts. Professionals should invest time in truly understanding others' goals, challenges, and contexts to build trust and genuine rapport.

In this section, we will look at why networking is essential to professional success. We will also examine the mindset shifts that separate surface level contact from meaningful connection, along with the practical actions needed to create and maintain a strong and varied network. We will also examine case examples and best practices that show how professionals at all levels can make networking a core competency, transforming it from an occasional task into a powerful, ongoing strategy for impact and growth.

The Case for Networking: Beyond Who You Know

The value of networking goes far beyond the familiar saying, "it's not what you know, it's who you know." While that phrase contains a grain of truth, it oversimplifies the real dynamic of professional success. In reality, success relies not only on what you know but also on the people you know, and most importantly on how you bring the two together in practice (Ibarra & Hunter, 2007). Your technical skills, experience, and knowledge form the foundation of your professional credibility and capability. But these qualifications alone mean little if they remain hidden or underutilized. To maximize their impact, you must apply them at scale, mobilize resources, secure buy-in for your ideas, discover new opportunities, and deliver results that matter. That is precisely where networking becomes indispensable.

A strong, diverse, and well-maintained network acts as a force multiplier for professional effectiveness by delivering multiple forms of value.

Access to Information: Networks expose you to critical insights about trends, opportunities, and challenges that you would not uncover in isolation. Conversations with peers, clients, or industry experts can reveal early signals about market shifts, evolving customer needs, or emerging technologies, helping you anticipate change and make better decisions (Granovetter, 1983).

Resource Leverage: Networking connects you to people who have expertise, tools, or influence that you may lack personally. Instead of being limited to what you can do alone, you can assemble the right resources to solve problems, develop new offerings, or advance strategic initiatives (Cross et al., 2016).

Opportunity Flow: Referrals, endorsements, and introductions often arise naturally from trust-based relationships. These connections can lead to new projects, partnerships, collaborations, or career opportunities that would remain closed otherwise (Higgins & Kram, 2001).

Professional Support: A solid network offers guidance, mentorship, and encouragement that sustain you through challenges. Experienced colleagues can help you navigate difficult decisions, avoid pitfalls, or develop new skills, making you more resilient and adaptable (Blau, 1964).

Collective Problem-Solving: Networking enables you to leverage diverse perspectives and experiences to tackle complex challenges. By bringing together people from different backgrounds, industries, or functions, you generate more creative and effective solutions than you could alone (Burt, 2004).

Without intentional networking, professionals risk becoming siloed, cut off from new ideas, and constrained by limited perspectives and resources. They may miss vital information, struggle to secure support for their initiatives, or fail to recognize emerging opportunities until it's too late. Networking is not about superficial socializing or transactional self-interest; it is about deliberately building a resilient web of trust- based relationships that enables you, and those around you, to achieve more together than any of you could alone. It is a core professional competency that supports sustained success, adaptability, and impact in an increasingly complex and interconnected world.

The Networking Mindset: Purposeful and Authentic

Adopting an effective networking mindset means rejecting the shallow, self-serving approach that many people associate with the term "networking." Too often, networking is dismissed as schmoozing at parties, collecting business cards with forced smiles, or amassing hundreds of LinkedIn connections without meaningful engagement. True professionals know that effective networking is far more valuable and sophisticated. It is the art of building genuine, lasting relationships that create shared value over time.

Connections are not transactions to be completed but relationships to be nurtured. Three critical qualities define this mindset:

Purposeful

Effective networking is intentional. It's not simply about being friendly or collecting contacts without a clear purpose. Professionals know what they want to achieve, whether that's gaining market insight, exploring collaboration, learning best practices, or building strategic alliances.

Example: A sustainability manager joins an industry consortium to learn about green supply chains. Instead of just swapping business cards, she asks focused questions about supplier audits, shares her own experiences with circular economy principles, and develops a partnership to create shared standards.

Authentic

Authentic networking is rooted in genuine interest and professional integrity. It's about being real, honest, and curious, showing up as yourself without pretense. This authenticity builds trust, the foundation of any long-lasting professional relationship.

Example: A junior analyst at a consulting firm meets a senior executive at an industry event. Instead of trying to impress, he asks sincere questions about the executive's career path and lessons learned. The executive appreciates the genuine curiosity and later agrees to mentor the analyst. Similarly, a salesperson who prioritizes understanding a client's goals over pushing a generic pitch builds stronger, more sustainable business relationships.

Mutual

Effective networking is built on mutual benefit. It is not about extracting value from others but about creating relationships where both sides can grow and succeed together.

Example: An HR director takes part in a roundtable with leaders from different industries focused on employee wellbeing. She openly shares her company's experiences from testing mental health programs, including where they fell short, and in return learns from peers about new approaches to digital wellness tools. She later recommends a colleague from another company for a role, and that colleague's organization reciprocates by sharing their onboarding framework. Likewise, a freelance designer who refs overflow work to peers finds they return the favor, creating a web of trust and opportunity for all involved.

A professional networking mindset reframes connection-building from a transactional act to an essential responsibility. It recognizes that in today's interconnected, fast-changing world, no one can succeed alone. Relationships built on purpose, authenticity, and mutual benefit become the infrastructure of success, enabling professionals to navigate complexity, innovate effectively, and deliver greater value to their organizations and communities.

Building a Networking Strategy

Networking is not a random or reactive activity. It is a deliberate and continuous practice that calls for the same level of planning and intention as any other professional project. Just as you wouldn't launch a major initiative without goals, timelines, or resources, you shouldn't approach networking without a strategy. Professionals who treat networking as a strategic discipline see far better results: stronger relationships, richer insights, and more sustained opportunities.

A well-designed networking strategy turns vague intentions into concrete action by providing a clear roadmap. Below is a structured approach to designing that strategy, with practical steps and considerations that professionals at any level can apply. To make this framework clearer, Figure 12 below illustrates the four key components of a professional networking strategy. Each step builds upon the previous one to help transform abstract intentions into a practical, sustainable roadmap.

1. Define Your Goals

The first and most critical step is achieving clarity: What do you want from your networking efforts? Without clear goals, it is easy to drift into superficial conversations or scatter your energy without impact.

Your goals might include:

- Expanding industry knowledge to anticipate trends ahead of competitors.
- Gaining visibility in a new market or role to establish yourself as a credible voice.
- Finding mentors or advisors who can accelerate your learning and development.
- Building partnerships for upcoming projects or strategic initiatives.
- Identifying talent to fill skill gaps or expand team capacity.

Clear goals ensure that every networking action you take is purposeful and aligned with what truly matters to your success.

BUILDING A NETWORKING STRATEGY

Networking isn't a random or reactive activity—It is a deliberate, ongoing practice that deserves the same level of planning and intention as any other professional project.

1 **DEFINE YOUR GOALS**

The first and most critical step is achieving clarity. What do you want from your networking efforts.

2 **MAP YOUR CURRENT NETWORK**

Networking isn't about knowing everyone—it is about knowing the right people and cultivating relationships

3 **IDENTIFY PRIORITY CONNECTIONS**

Networking isn't about knowing everyone— it is about knowing the right people and cultivating relationships that truly matter

4 **PLAN YOUR ENGAGEMENT**

Consistent and thoughtful engagement is essential to building strong relationships:

- Attending industry events, conferences, or webinars
- Joining professional associations or online communit
- Scheduling regular time each week or month for outreach and frior–up

Figure 12: A Four-Step Framework for Building a Networking Strategy

143

2. Map Your Current Network

Once you know your goals, assess your current standing. Mapping your network helps you understand your strengths and identify critical gaps.

Consider:

- Who is already in your network? Include colleagues, mentors, partners, industry peers, past clients, alumni, and professional acquaintances.
- Where are the gaps? Are you missing connections in certain industries, regions, areas of expertise, or levels of influence?
- Who do you need to know to achieve your goals?

This reflective exercise prevents you from defaulting to your comfort zone and ensures your network is strategically constructed rather than accidental.

3. Identify Priority Connections

Networking is not about trying to know everyone. It is about building relationships with the right people and focusing on the connections that genuinely matter. This means prioritizing outreach intentionally.

Focus on:

- High-value contacts who can provide critical insight, resources, or support aligned with your goals.
- Diverse contacts who bring different perspectives, backgrounds, or industry knowledge, helping you avoid echo chambers.
- Potential champions or connectors who can introduce you to others and expand your reach.

Prioritizing strategically ensures that your limited time and energy are invested where they will deliver the most meaningful returns.

4. Plan Your Engagement

Networking is not a one-time task but an ongoing practice. Consistent and thoughtful engagement is essential to maintain authentic and productive relationships. Key elements of an engagement plan include:

- Attending industry events, conferences, or webinars to meet peers, learn trends, and raise your profile.
- Joining professional associations or online communities to access curated groups of like-minded professionals.
- Scheduling regular time each week or month to reach out, follow up, and maintain existing relationships.
- Sharing useful content, whether it is an article, an insight, or an introduction, keeps you visible while offering real value to others.

This intentional approach turns passive contacts into active, trust-based relationships.

Case Study: Building a Networking Strategy in Action

Consider Li Wei, a mid-level project manager in the construction industry, aiming to transition into executive leadership with a focus on sustainable building practices. Recognizing that technical expertise alone is not enough, Li Wei designs a structured networking strategy to build the right relationships, access critical knowledge, and establish his credibility in the green construction space.

Step 1: Define Goals

Li Wei's goals are clear and tailored to his career shift:

- Learning about the latest green building technologies and regulations.
- Gaining visibility and credibility among sustainability-focused developers and architects.
- Finding mentors with experience in large-scale green projects.
- Building partnerships with suppliers of eco-friendly construction materials.

By defining specific goals, Li Wei ensures every networking activity is aligned and purposeful.

Step 2: Map His Current Network

Li Wei audits his existing relationships:

- Strong ties to local government inspectors and traditional contractors.
- Few contacts in sustainability-focused design firms or consultancies.
- No meaningful relationships with eco-material suppliers or environmental consultants.

This mapping reveals that his current network is too traditional and lacks the necessary sustainability expertise.

Step 3: Identify Priority Connections

With goals and gaps in mind, Li Wei prioritizes:

- Senior sustainability consultants who can mentor him.
- Architects are renowned for green building design.
- Suppliers of eco-friendly construction materials.
- Leaders of industry associations in green building.

He researches these groups and identifies key people and organizations to target.

Step 4: Plan Engagement

Li Wei develops a clear engagement plan:

- Registering for two leading green-building conferences where his target contacts will be present.
- Joining a professional association for sustainable construction.
- Setting biweekly calendar reminders to engage on LinkedIn, commenting on posts, and building rapport.
- Following up with new contacts after events with personalized emails or coffee invitations.
- Sharing industry articles and case studies to demonstrate his expertise and add value.

Within six months, this intentional strategy delivers clear, career-shaping results:

- He secures two mentors with deep sustainability experience who offer invaluable guidance.
- He is invited to speak on a panel about integrating sustainable practices into mid-sized projects.
- He develops a partnership with a supplier of recycled building materials, giving his firm a competitive edge.

Li Wei's story shows that networking is not about luck or guesswork. It is a focused and disciplined strategy. By defining goals, mapping his network, identifying priority connections, and planning his engagement, he transforms his career trajectory while building authentic, mutually valuable relationships.

This structured approach is a model any professional can use. Whether you're an early-career specialist seeking mentorship, a manager expanding into new markets, or an executive seeking strategic alliances, a thoughtful networking strategy can turn vague intentions into concrete, sustainable success.

Sustaining Relationships Over Time

Networking doesn't end the moment you exchange business cards, have a coffee meeting, or connect on LinkedIn. That first introduction is only the beginning. The true value of networking lies in sustaining relationships over time, transforming initial contacts into genuine, enduring professional connections that deepen and evolve along with your career (Ibarra & Hunter, 2007; Uzzi & Dunlap, 2005).

Strong networks don't maintain themselves automatically. They require intentional, consistent effort that shows you care about the relationship, not just what you can get from it (Blau, 1964). Professionals who master this see enormous returns: they build trust, strengthen their reputation, and become the kind of person others want to work with, recommend, and support in return.

Here are four essential practices for maintaining resilient professional relationships over time:

Follow Up

One of the simplest and most overlooked ways to stand out professionally is to follow up thoughtfully after meeting someone. Instead of letting a good conversation fade into memory, take time to thank the person and reinforce the connection.

For example, after meeting a peer at a conference, you might send a short, personalized email:

"I really enjoyed our conversation about sustainable design trends. Here's that article I mentioned, I think you'll find it valuable."

These small gestures demonstrate professionalism, attention to detail, and genuine interest in the other person's success. They also help establish a pattern of reliable, respectful communication that builds trust over time.

Stay in Touch

Relationships often fade because people only reach out when they need something. Proactive contact that expects nothing in return demonstrates genuine respect and value for the relationship itself.

You might check in every few months with a friendly message:

"I saw your company just launched its new product, congratulations! How have things been on your end?"

Such low-key, friendly outreach keeps you on their radar and reminds them you see them as a colleague, not just a resource to exploit.

Offer Help

True networking is reciprocal. One of the most powerful ways to sustain relationships is to look for opportunities to help others, even when there's no immediate benefit to you.

You might introduce a former colleague to someone hiring in your network, share insights on a new market trend they're exploring, or offer to review a proposal they're working on. These small acts of generosity build significant goodwill over time and position you as a trusted, reliable professional.

Be Visible

Remaining active and visible in your professional circles is another way to sustain relationships, even with people you don't speak to regularly. Staying visible in your network comes from regularly offering value, whether through sharing helpful content, joining conversations, or speaking at industry events..

For instance, you might:

- Write short LinkedIn posts about lessons learned on recent projects.
- Speak on a panel at a local industry meetup.
- Participate actively in professional association forums.

By consistently "showing up," you remind your network of your expertise and values, making it easier for people to reach out, collaborate with you, or recommend you when opportunities arise.

Professionals who take the time to nurture their relationships create more than just a list of contacts. They build a lasting reputation. Over time, you become known as someone generous, reliable, and engaged: someone who invests in others, delivers on promises, and strengthens the professional community around them.

This reputation compounds over the years, creating a network of people who trust you, respect you, and advocate for you even when you're not in the room. In today's interconnected and collaborative world, this is more than an advantage. It is the foundation for lasting professional success.

Section 2: Collaboration – Achieving More Together

Strategic networking expands your professional reach, giving you access to new ideas, resources, and relationships. But its actual value is realized only when those connections evolve into meaningful collaboration. Collaboration is the discipline that transforms a network of contacts into a team of allies working toward shared goals. It is the art and science of combining diverse skills, experiences, and perspectives to achieve outcomes no one could accomplish alone (Gray, 1989). In today's fast-moving, interconnected world, collaboration is not optional, it is essential (Cross et al., 2016).

Complex challenges rarely yield to individual effort. Organizations today operate in environments marked by rapid change, high interdependence, and increasing complexity (Heifetz & Linsky, 2002). Success demands the ability to coordinate seamlessly across functions, disciplines, organizations, and even industries. Collaboration is what enables professionals to deliver integrated solutions, innovate effectively, and meet the evolving expectations of stakeholders and customers (Edmondson & Harvey, 2017).

Despite its importance, collaboration often fails to live up to its promise. Teams that should work together seamlessly can become mired in conflict, poor communication, or misaligned priorities (Jehn & Mannix, 2001). Departments may retreat into silos, prioritizing their own interests over shared goals (Lawrence & Lorsch, 1967). Individuals may resist sharing credit or information, fearing they will lose influence or recognition (Edmondson, 2012). Even well-intentioned professionals can struggle to coordinate effectively when working across different disciplines, organizations, or cultures.

These challenges do not occur because people lack concern. They arise when collaboration is treated as something casual instead of being approached as a structured and intentional process. Effective collaboration requires far more than goodwill or ad-hoc cooperation. It demands clarity, discipline, and a shared commitment to collective success.

Professionals who master collaboration don't just deliver better results for their organizations, they also strengthen their reputations as reliable partners, effective leaders, and valuable problem-solvers. They become known for their ability to bring people together, align efforts, and deliver on shared goals, even in complex or challenging environments.

This section offers a practical roadmap for transitioning from superficial cooperation to disciplined, high- value collaboration. You will learn how to establish shared goals that align teams, define clear roles and responsibilities to ensure accountability, create open communication channels that build understanding and trust, and manage conflict productively to turn potential friction into creative solutions. You'll also explore practical tools, from collaboration charters to structured feedback loops, that help embed these practices in your day-to-day work.

By applying these principles, you can transform collaboration from a vague aspiration into a repeatable, reliable driver of professional and organizational excellence. You will not only achieve better outcomes for your team and your organization but also build the kind of trust, credibility, and influence that expands your professional opportunities.

Foundations of Effective Collaboration

Collaboration is not something casual or improvised. It is a structured and intentional discipline that allows professionals with different expertise to coordinate their efforts and achieve outcomes that no individual or isolated group could accomplish on their own (Edmondson & Harvey, 2017).

Without deliberate foundations in place, teams quickly slip into misalignment, duplicated work, poor communication, or unresolved conflicts, which can derail outcomes (Jehn & Mannix, 2001). High-performing teams recognize that effective collaboration demands design, discipline, and ongoing attention (Cross et al., 2016).

Structured collaboration practices, such as clear goal setting, defined roles and responsibilities, open communication channels, and conflict management processes, help teams navigate complexity and maintain alignment even in dynamic environments. By investing in these foundations, organizations can turn collaboration from a vague aspiration into a repeatable driver of innovation, efficiency, and shared success.

Below is a roadmap of **four essential foundations** of effective collaboration, demonstrated through a single, evolving example of a cross-functional product launch team putting these principles into practice.

1. Shared Goals and Purpose

Collaboration begins with establishing a clear, shared purpose. Without a common goal, teams drift, work at cross purposes, or focus narrowly on departmental priorities at the expense of overall success.

Principle: Align everyone around what they're trying to achieve, and why it matters.

Best practices include:

- Defining clear, measurable, time-bound objectives.
- Articulating the strategic importance of the goal.
- Ensuring buy-in from all participants.

Example:

A technology company is launching a new customer platform. Initially, engineering, marketing, and customer support teams all pursued their own objectives: engineers focused on features, marketing on messaging, and support on training. Frustration built as deadlines slipped and work conflicted.

To address this, leadership convened a cross-functional kickoff workshop. Together, the teams defined their shared purpose: "Deliver a fully integrated, customer-ready platform in six months to capture a critical market window." This purpose was made explicit, documented, and widely communicated, providing everyone with a unifying mission that explained not only what to do but also why it mattered.

2. Role Clarity and Responsibility

Even with shared goals, collaboration falters if people don't know who is responsible for what. Ambiguity leads to duplication, gaps, and conflict.

Principle: Ensure everyone knows their role, understands their responsibilities, and sees how their work connects to others.

Best practices include:

- Clearly defining and documenting roles.
- Using frameworks like **DACI** to make decision rights explicit, where the **Driver** coordinates and pushes work forward, the **Approver** has final decision authority, **Contributors** provide expertise and complete tasks, and **Informed** stakeholders are kept updated on progress.
- Regularly revisiting roles as the project evolves.

Example:

After agreeing on the shared goal, the team tackled confusion over responsibilities. They used the DACI Model to assign clear roles (See figure 13):

- **Driver:** The Product Manager coordinated timelines and dependencies.
- **Approver:** The Head of Product had the final say on scope changes.
- **Contributors:** Engineering delivered features, Marketing created launch materials, Customer Support developed training.
- **Informed:** Executive Leadership received regular updates.

By clearly mapping these roles, the team avoided duplicated work, reduced miscommunication about ownership, and expedited decision-making, thereby building trust across departments.

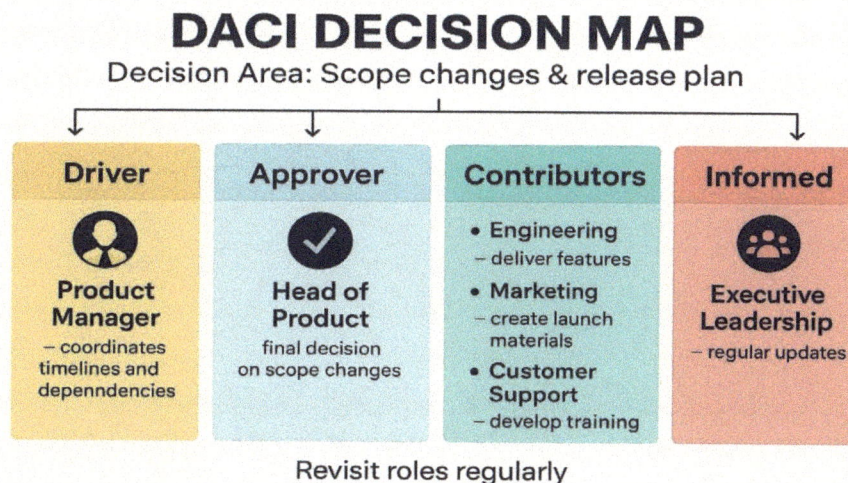

Figure 13: DACI Decision Map – Role Clarity for Scope Changes & Release Planning

3. Open and Constructive Communication

Collaboration flourishes when communication is clear, timely, and respectful. Without it, even well-planned projects break down.

Principle: Establish regular, structured communication to ensure alignment and build trust.

Best practices include:

- Scheduling routine check-ins with clear agendas.
- Using shared dashboards or tools for real-time visibility.
- Encouraging respectful dialogue and active listening.
- Creating a psychological safety culture so that issues can be raised early.

Example:

With shared goals and roles in place, the team recognized they still needed better day-to-day coordination. They instituted weekly stand-up meetings where teams reported progress, flagged risks, and adjusted plans collaboratively.

They also adopted a shared project management dashboard for complete visibility into tasks and timelines. Rules for respectful, constructive discussion were agreed upon. As a result, potential bottlenecks were spotted early, surprises were kept to a minimum, and team members felt acknowledged and valued.

4. Managing Conflict Productively

Conflict is inevitable when people with different priorities and expertise collaborate. However, when managed effectively, conflict is not destructive, it is productive, leading to better ideas and more informed decisions.

Principle: Channel conflict into respectful, goal-focused debate that strengthens outcomes.

Best practices include:

- Establishing norms for respectful disagreement.
- Keeping discussions focused on ideas, not personalities.
- Grounding debates in shared goals.
- Using facilitators for especially sensitive issues.

Example:

Midway through the project, conflict emerged over scope: Engineering wanted to cut features to meet deadlines, while Marketing insisted those features were critical for customer appeal.

Instead of letting the disagreement fester, the Product Manager facilitated a structured workshop. They reviewed the shared goal of launching a customer-ready platform in six months and openly debated trade-offs. By focusing on customer value and launch timing as the guiding priorities, they reached a compromise on a phased release plan that satisfied both sides.

Conflict wasn't removed; instead, it was handled productively, which helped strengthen the solution.

By focusing on shared goals, clear roles, open communication, and effective conflict management, the cross-functional team transformed a potential disaster into a successful launch.

They didn't just avoid failure, they built a collaborative culture that improved trust, accelerated decision- making, and delivered real business value.

These four foundations aren't theoretical, they are practical, proven steps any team can use to transform collaboration from a buzzword into a reliable driver of professional excellence and organizational success.

Tools for Structured Collaboration

Collaboration doesn't succeed on good intentions alone, it thrives on structure. Even the most committed teams can stumble without clear agreements, regular check-ins, and shared expectations.

Structured collaboration tools help embed the principles of effective teamwork into daily practice, making alignment, accountability, and continuous improvement part of how the team works, not just something they hope for.

Below are two proven tools that bring discipline and clarity to collaboration, enabling diverse professionals to work together to achieve shared goals truly.

1. Collaboration Charter

A Collaboration Charter is a living, written agreement that acts as the team's contract for how they will work together. Far from being bureaucratic, it is a powerful tool that sets the stage for success by forcing the team to have critical conversations up front (Gray, 2016).

It helps align everyone on purpose, roles, norms, and processes before misunderstandings, assumptions, or conflicts have a chance to derail progress. It also serves as a reference point to revisit when tensions arise or priorities shift.

Key sections in a Collaboration Charter typically include:

- **Purpose and Objectives:** Why does this team exist? What shared goals are they working toward?
- **Team Membership and Roles:** Who is involved, and what are each person's responsibilities? This reduces confusion and overlap.
- **Communication Norms and Meeting Cadence:** How often will the team meet? What channels will they use? What are the expectations for responsiveness and transparency?
- **Decision-Making Processes:** How will the team make key choices? Who has final approval?
- **Conflict Resolution Processes:** How will disagreements be surfaced and resolved constructively?

The Collaboration Charter, as illustrated in Figure 14, serves as a practical example of how a cross-functional team can ensure shared goals, clear roles, and seamless coordination. It defines a Purpose and Objectives section, committing the team to collaboratively design, build, and launch a new customer platform within six months to support strategic growth by expanding market share by 15%.

The Team Membership and Roles section outlines responsibilities, from the Product Manager overseeing timelines to contributors like Engineering, Marketing, and Customer Support Leads.

Communication Norms and Meeting Cadence outline structured interactions, including weekly stand-ups, biweekly planning sessions, and transparent sharing of risks. Decision-Making Processes detail how input is gathered, approvals are secured, and trade-offs are resolved. Finally, the Team Commitment emphasizes maintaining alignment, trust, and accountability throughout the project, creating a clear, shared framework for effective collaboration.

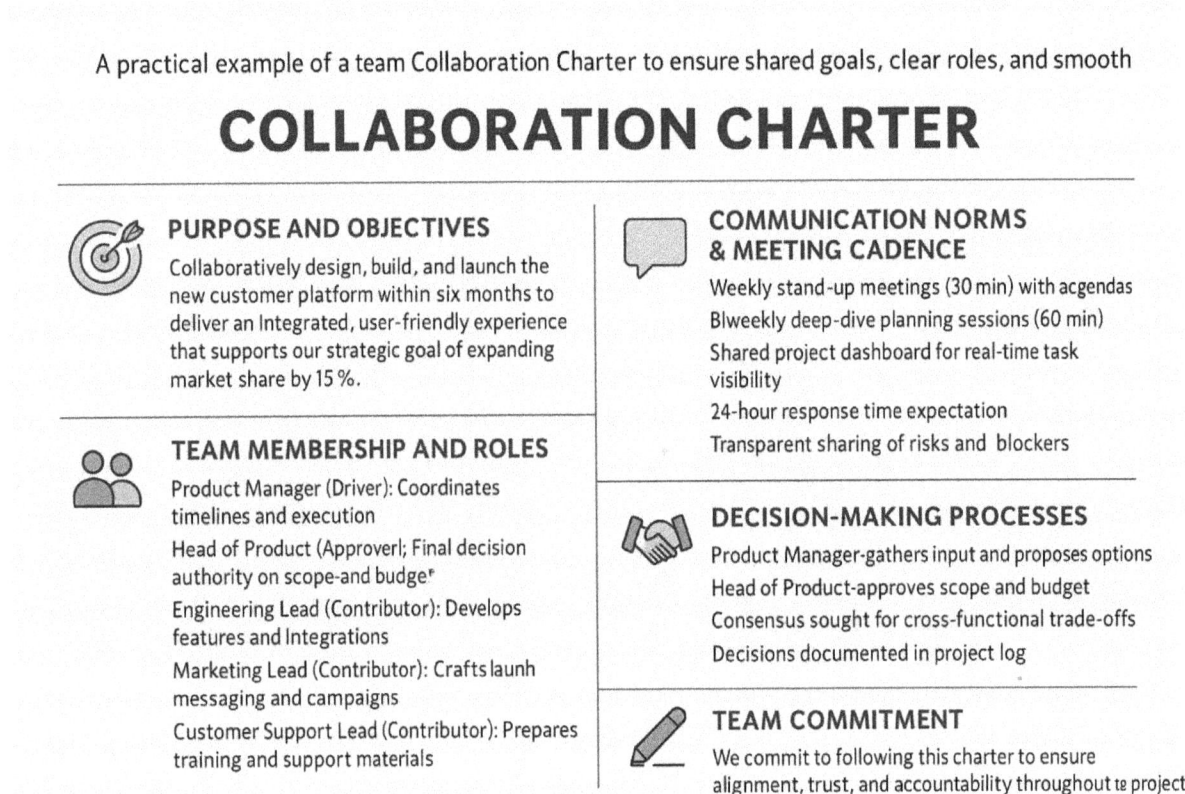

A practical example of a team Collaboration Charter to ensure shared goals, clear roles, and smooth

COLLABORATION CHARTER

PURPOSE AND OBJECTIVES

Collaboratively design, build, and launch the new customer platform within six months to deliver an Integrated, user-friendly experience that supports our strategic goal of expanding market share by 15%.

TEAM MEMBERSHIP AND ROLES

Product Manager (Driver): Coordinates timelines and execution

Head of Product (Approverl; Final decision authority on scope-and budge⁴

Engineering Lead (Contributor): Develops features and Integrations

Marketing Lead (Contributor): Crafts launh messaging and campaigns

Customer Support Lead (Contributor): Prepares training and support materials

COMMUNICATION NORMS & MEETING CADENCE

Weekly stand-up meetings (30 min) with acgendas

BIweekly deep-dive planning sessions (60 min)

Shared project dashboard for real-time task visibility

24-hour response time expectation

Transparent sharing of risks and blockers

DECISION-MAKING PROCESSES

Product Manager-gathers input and proposes options

Head of Product-approves scope and budget

Consensus sought for cross-functional trade-offs

Decisions documented in project log

TEAM COMMITMENT

We commit to following this charter to ensure alignment, trust, and accountability throughout te project

Figure 14: The Collaboration Charter

Creating a charter together is more than filling out a form. It is a shared design exercise that fosters trust, reveals hidden assumptions, and aligns the team from the outset. When everyone understands and agrees to how they will collaborate, they can focus on delivering results rather than navigating confusion or turf battles.

2. Feedback Loops

Effective collaboration is not fixed; it evolves as circumstances shift and teams gain new insights. That's why Feedback Loops are essential: they enable teams to improve, adapt, and stay aligned continuously.

Feedback loops provide a structured way to share observations, raise issues early, and identify ways to work more effectively together. Rather than waiting for problems to blow up, teams use feedback as a regular, proactive practice (Argyris & Schön, 1996).

Key forms of feedback loops include:

- **Regular Retrospectives:** Scheduled sessions (often at key project milestones or intervals) where the team reflects on what's working well, what isn't, and what adjustments are needed. This creates a culture of continuous improvement.
- **One-on-One Check-Ins:** Individual conversations between team members or with the leader to address concerns early, offer support, and strengthen relationships. These reduce the risk of issues festering quietly.
- **Open Forums:** Group discussions or online spaces where team members can share ideas, voice concerns, or suggest improvements in real time.

Real-Life Example: Feedback Loops in Action

The marketing team at InnovateCo was tasked with launching a major new product in a highly competitive market. The stakes were high: missing the deadline or misreading customer needs could cost them their market advantage.

Initially, the team relied solely on weekly status meetings. But problems kept surfacing too late. Designers and copywriters felt that their input wasn't being heard, analytics teams were unclear on goals, and the project manager was constantly firefighting miscommunications.

Realizing they needed a better way to stay aligned, they implemented structured feedback loops into their collaboration process.

Regular Retrospectives:

After each key milestone, such as completing initial campaign concepts or finalizing ad copy, the entire team held retrospectives. These weren't simple status updates; they were open, structured conversations about what worked, what didn't, and how to improve.

For example, after the first creative review, they realized approvals were too slow because feedback wasn't consolidated. In the retrospective, they agreed on a single review document and more precise deadlines for stakeholder input. This simple change cut review time by 40% on the next round.

One-on-One Check-Ins:

The marketing manager also scheduled monthly one-on-one check-ins with each team member.

In these private conversations, people felt safe raising concerns early, such as feeling overwhelmed with revisions or being unclear about campaign priorities. The manager could offer targeted support, reassign work to balance loads, and clear up misunderstandings before they escalated into team-wide problems.

These check-ins fostered trust and demonstrated that feedback wasn't just for the team; it was personal and encouraging.

Open Forums:

Beyond retrospectives and private check-ins, the team created an open forum in their project chat app, a dedicated channel called #campaign-feedback.

Here, anyone could suggest ideas, raise potential risks, or share customer insights as they emerged. For instance, the social media lead shared early feedback that customers were confused about the new pricing model. This surfaced weeks earlier than it would have through formal reporting, allowing the messaging team to adjust their materials before launch.

The Impact:

By adopting these **feedback loops,** retrospectives, one-on-ones, and open forums, InnovateCo's marketing team turned reactive problem-solving into proactive alignment.

They reduced miscommunication, increased transparency, and fostered a culture of psychological safety where people felt comfortable admitting mistakes and suggesting improvements. The end result was not just an on- time launch but one with messaging and creative that was stronger because it was shaped by continuous learning and open collaboration.

Feedback loops enabled the team to shift from a one-time plan to an ongoing, adaptive conversation, fostering a culture where learning and improvement became a shared, continuous habit.

Section 3: Value Exchange – Creating Mutual Benefit

In today's interconnected and interdependent professional world, building a strong network and collaborating effectively are crucial. However, they alone are not enough to guarantee lasting success. True professional excellence depends on mastering value exchange: the practice of creating, delivering, and recognizing mutual benefit in every interaction (Kotler & Keller, 2015; Uzzi, 1997).

Value exchange is what transforms transactional, one-off encounters into durable, high-trust partnerships. It moves relationships from opportunistic deals to sustained alliances that deliver compounding advantages over time. Professionals and organizations that truly grasp value exchange don't merely focus on what they can gain from others. They think critically about what they can create together (Lencioni, 2002).

This principle isn't abstract. It's about adopting a mindset that actively seeks to understand others' goals, challenges, and pressures, then working creatively and generously to find shared solutions. At its core, value exchange asks:

"What can we accomplish together?" rather than "What can I get from you?"

This shift in thinking is decisive because it turns clients, colleagues, and partners from mere resources into genuine stakeholders. It reframes professional interactions as opportunities to serve, support, and empower one another, laying the groundwork for relationships that are not just deep and resilient but also mutually rewarding (Grant, 2013).

This is the difference that value exchange makes. It turns shallow contact lists into genuine communities of trust. It ensures that when opportunities appear, you are not seen merely as a vendor but as a partner.

Organizations that practice value exchange strategically see similar benefits. They don't compete solely on cost or convenience; instead, they create ecosystems of loyalty where customers, suppliers, and collaborators all have incentives to help one another succeed (Porter & Kramer, 2011).

Professionals who internalize the discipline of value exchange also build reputations that compound over time. They are seen as reliable partners, creative problem-solvers, and indispensable collaborators who consistently make others better, faster, and more successful.

This section will explore how to move from a mindset of transaction to one of sustained, mutual value. You'll learn how to understand what others truly need, how to deliver relevant and meaningful value, and how to ensure that value is visible and acknowledged.

We'll also explore the principle of reciprocity, which is the natural human tendency to return favors and share opportunities with those who help us first, and how to practice it authentically.

Finally, you'll discover practical tools for embedding value exchange in your professional routine, from stakeholder mapping to mutual benefit agreements, so you can systematically transform your interactions into engines of growth, trust, and opportunity.

The Value Exchange Mindset

Adopting value exchange as a professional discipline is not about adding a simple tactic to your approach, it demands a fundamental shift in perspective and intention. It's the move from transactional thinking to building meaningful, trust-based partnerships that deliver sustained, mutual value over time.

Professionals who adopt this mindset recognize that strong relationships are not formed through opportunistic, one-off requests. Instead, they invest in building long-term connections, recognizing that consistent engagement and support can transform brief encounters into enduring partnerships.

From Transaction to Relationship:

Avoid the mindset that treats every interaction as a quick win or a one-time exchange. Instead, prioritize building relationships that will deliver value repeatedly over time. This means staying in touch even when you don't need anything, showing genuine interest, and being someone others can rely on beyond any immediate opportunity.

From Self-Interest to Mutual Benefit:

Shift your focus away from simply advancing your own goals. Make it your practice to truly understand and support the needs, goals, and challenges of others. Ask: What does this person need? How can I help them succeed? This kind of empathy not only strengthens individual relationships but also positions you as a collaborative partner that others are eager to work with.

From Scarcity to Abundance:

Reject the notion that sharing knowledge, credit, or opportunities diminishes your own value. Embrace the idea that value grows when it's shared. When you offer insights freely, make helpful introductions, or celebrate others' contributions, you don't lose your advantage, you build trust, earn goodwill, and create professional environments where everyone can thrive.

This mindset shift is not simply about being "nice" or altruistic. It is a professional strategy grounded in reality: people are drawn to those who make them better, solve their problems, and care about their success.

Professional Reflection:

Consider how you approach your networking opportunities. Are you scanning the room, looking for people who can help you get ahead? Or are you seeking ways to connect people, solve problems, and make introductions that benefit everyone?

The first approach might give you a stack of business cards. The second helps build a reputation for being generous, a strong leader, and trustworthy, making you someone others want to collaborate with, recommend, and support in return.

Adopting the value exchange mindset doesn't mean ignoring your own goals. It means achieving them in a more sustainable, ethical, and ultimately successful way by making yourself indispensable to others' success.

Principles of Effective Value Exchange

1. Understand What Others Value

You can't deliver value if you don't know what your partners care about. This requires curiosity, empathy, and active listening. Ask questions to uncover their goals, challenges, and success criteria.

- What are their priorities?
- What pressures or constraints do they face?
- How do they define success?
- What would make them look good to their own stakeholders?

Professional Example:

Consider a software account manager who wants to move beyond simply fulfilling orders to becoming a trusted partner for her clients. Instead of immediately pitching features, she takes the time to understand what her client truly values most.

She begins by meeting with stakeholders from different teams in the client organization and asking thoughtful, open-ended questions:

- **"What are your top priorities over the next year?"**
  She learns that their leadership is laser-focused on reducing customer churn, which is cutting into revenue and growth targets.

- **"What pressures or constraints are you facing in reaching that goal?"**
  They explain that their support team is stretched thin, customer training resources are outdated, and churn tends to spike when users don't understand the software's advanced features.

- **"How do you define success?"**
  The client team describes success as lowering churn by at least 15% over the next two quarters while maintaining customer satisfaction scores.

- **"What would make you look good to your stakeholders?"**
  Managers share that they need to show measurable improvements in user engagement and retention metrics to secure next year's budget and demonstrate ROI to executives.

Armed with these insights, the account manager tailors her approach to deliver real, relevant value. Instead of pushing generic training packages or one-size-fits-all support plans, she co-designs a customized program:

Advanced reporting features are emphasized during deployment, allowing the client to track churn risks in real-time.

- Targeted training sessions are developed for the client's specific high-risk user groups.
- Self-service resources are enhanced to alleviate the support team's workload.
- A shared dashboard is set up to monitor progress toward the 15% reduction in churn goal.

By aligning her solution with the client's true priorities, overcoming their pressures, supporting their success criteria, and helping them shine internally, she moves from being a vendor to becoming an indispensable partner.

The result? The client reduces churn by 20%, renews the software contract at an expanded scope, and cites the account manager's consultative approach as a key reason for their success.

2. Offer Real, Relevant Value

Once you understand what matters to others, the next step is to deliver. This doesn't always mean grand gestures or costly solutions. Value can take many forms:

- Sharing expertise or insights.
- Making introductions to valuable contacts.
- Solving a problem or removing a barrier.
- Sharing tools, resources, or best practices.
- Simply listening and offering perspective.

Professional Example:

After carefully uncovering her client's real priorities, which were reducing customer churn and improving user engagement, the Software Account Manager knew that simply listing product features or offering standard training packages wouldn't be enough. She needed to offer real, relevant value tailored to the client's unique needs and constraints.

Instead of pushing off-the-shelf solutions, she applied her understanding in practical, targeted ways:

- **Sharing expertise and insights:** She analyzed the client's churn data with them, highlighting user behavior trends and showing how advanced reporting features could predict at-risk accounts.
- **Solving a problem:** Recognizing the overstretched support team, she proposed easy-to-deploy self- service tutorials and FAQs that empowered customers to solve common issues without draining staff time.
- **Providing tailored resources:** She worked with her company's training team to customize learning modules specifically for the client's high-risk user segments, ensuring that training addressed the real gaps that were driving churn.
- **Offering perspective:** In meetings with the client's leadership, she openly discussed best practices from other successful deployments, helping them see opportunities they hadn't considered.

Her approach wasn't about grand, expensive add-ons, it was about listening carefully and then delivering practical, high-impact solutions that made the client's life easier, their results better, and their internal success more visible.

By doing so, she didn't just fulfill her role as an account manager. She became a trusted advisor, someone who consistently delivered real value in ways that mattered most to the client's business.

3. Make Value Visible and Acknowledged

Even when value is delivered, it can be overlooked or underappreciated if it's not visible. Professionals need to ensure value is recognized, not out of ego, but to reinforce trust and build momentum. Best practices include:

- Documenting and sharing outcomes.
- Celebrating joint wins.
- Offering sincere, specific recognition to partners.
- Reporting progress to stakeholders clearly and consistently.

Professional Example:

Delivering real value is only part of the equation. The Software Account Manager also knew that for her partnership to thrive, she needed to make that value visible and acknowledged, not to seek personal credit, but to reinforce trust, strengthen buy-in, and build lasting momentum.

She did this thoughtfully and deliberately:

- **Documenting and sharing outcomes:** After implementing the tailored training modules and self-service resources, she provided the client with clear, data-driven reports showing improvements in user engagement and a measurable decline in churn rates.
- **Celebrating joint wins:** In review meetings, she didn't just present numbers. She emphasized the client team's commitment and collaboration, framing the success as a shared achievement rather than a vendor-delivered service.
- **Offering sincere, specific recognition:** She made a point to personally thank the client's support and training leads for their insights and hard work, acknowledging their expertise and contributions during group calls and in follow-up emails.
- **Reporting progress consistently:** Rather than waiting for quarterly reviews, she established a cadence of brief, clear updates to keep stakeholders informed of results and next steps. This transparency-built confidence that improvements weren't one-off events, but part of a sustained, strategic partnership.

By ensuring that the value she delivered was both visible and recognized, the account manager did more than solve problems. She deepened trust, strengthened the client relationship, and positioned herself and her company as indispensable partners in the client's ongoing success.

The Reciprocity Principle

At the heart of value exchange is reciprocity. People are naturally inclined to return favors, share information, and support those who have helped them (Gouldner, 1960). But reciprocity is most powerful when it is intentional, consistent, and based on genuine interest in mutual benefit, rather than on short-term self-interest or transactional thinking (Grant, 2013).

Therefore, reciprocity is most powerful when it is:

- **Generous:** Give without immediately expecting something in return.
- **Consistent:** Make delivering value a habit, not a tactic.
- **Authentic:** Offer help sincerely, not manipulatively.

This principle turns connections into lasting partnerships built on trust (See figure 15).

THE RECIPROCITY PRINCIPLE

Value exchange thrives on intentional, consistent, genuine reciprocity.

Generous
Give without immediately expecting something in in return.

Consistent
Make delivering value a habit. not a tactic.

Authentic
Offer help sincerely, not manipulatively.

GIVING → PARTNERSHIP → REFERRALS

Share relevant insights, introductions, tools without expectation

Build mutual trust; co-créate value; keep promises

Aovocacy & introductions; renewals & expansions.

Give first. Give often. Give sincerely.

Figure 15: The Reciprocity Principle

Professional Example:

The Software Account Manager didn't wait for contract renewals to prove her value. Even outside formal projects, she regularly shared industry insights, offered quick tips to improve adoption, and connected clients to peers tackling similar challenges.

Because she consistently offered help with authenticity and generosity, expecting nothing in return, clients didn't just renew their contracts. They recommended her to others and turned to her first for new initiatives.

Tools for Practicing Value Exchange

Building strong, enduring partnerships doesn't happen by accident. Even the most well-intentioned professionals can fall short if they don't approach value exchange in a structured, deliberate way.

Practicing value exchange effectively requires moving beyond good intentions to clear planning and communication. Professionals who excel at this don't simply hope their partners recognize the value. They ensure it is clear, planned, and mutually understood (Brown & Wyatt, 2010).

Two essential tools facilitate this approach: Stakeholder Value Maps and Mutual Benefit Agreements. Used effectively, these tools help ensure that expectations are aligned, contributions are meaningful, and both parties walk away with clear, measurable value.

Stakeholder Value Map

A Stakeholder Value Map is a straightforward but powerful planning tool that helps professionals systematically understand and plan for the needs of their partners.

Instead of relying on assumptions or surface-level goals, it forces you to get specific about:

- Who your key stakeholders are.
- What they value most.
- How can you deliver that value?
- What you might need in return.

By mapping these elements, professionals can design tailored solutions that resonate with partners' real priorities, rather than offering generic support.

Example:

The account manager at a software firm used this approach to plan a client success strategy. She identified key stakeholders on the client side, such as the Head of Customer Success, Support Team Lead, and Marketing Director.

For each, she clarified:

- **Priorities:** Reducing customer churn, decreasing support ticket volume, and boosting adoption of advanced features.
- **Value She Could Offer:** Customized training for high-risk users, advanced reporting dashboards, self-service resources.
- **Her Ask or Need:** Early access to usage data, time from subject-matter experts to co-create training content.

STAKEHOLDER VALUE MAP

- Who your key stakeholders are.
- What they value most.
- How you can deliver that value.
- What you might need in return

Stakeholder	Their Priorities	Value I Can Offer	My Ask or Need
Head of Customer Success	Reduce churn to <15%	Advanced reporting, customized training	Usage data, training particip-
Support Team Lead	Lower ticket volume	Self-service resources, FAQs	Insights on top support issues
Marketing Director	Showcase product adoption	User success stories data analysis	Permission to use customer quotes

By making this map explicit, she ensured her proposed plan wasn't just well-intentioned, it was directly aligned with what each stakeholder cared about most, making buy-in far easier.

Mutual Benefit Agreements

Even the best plans can fail if expectations aren't clear. Mutual Benefit Agreements, whether formal contracts or informal written understandings, make sure both sides are aligned on how they will support each other.

These agreements outline shared goals, clarify what each party will contribute, and define timelines and key performance indicators (KPIs). They help avoid confusion, minimize conflict, and make sure both sides know exactly what to expect.

Example (Software Account Manager):

Once she mapped stakeholder needs and offered tailored solutions, the account manager formalized the partnership in an internal agreement. She outlined:

- **Shared Goals:** Reduce churn by 15%, improve adoption of advanced features.

164

- **Contributions:** Client team would provide early access to usage data and allocate time for feedback. The software company would deliver customized training modules, advanced reporting dashboards, and regular progress reviews.
- **Timelines and Success Measures:** Agreed milestones for training deployment and quarterly reviews of churn and usage metrics.

This approach ensured both sides understood their roles and commitments clearly, reducing misunderstandings and reinforcing accountability.

By using Stakeholder Value Maps and Mutual Benefit Agreements, professionals move from hoping to deliver value to planning and proving it. These tools help turn abstract ideas about value exchange into real, shared, and sustained success.

Executive Snapshot – Chapter 5: Strategic Connection

Strategic Connection turns individual competence into collective advantage. Mapping stakeholders, offering value first, and nurturing diverse networks multiplies both opportunity and insight. Relationships thrive on thoughtful reciprocity and disciplined follow-through. The following recap helps you embed networking as a systematic, value-driven practice rather than a sporadic activity.

- ✓ Map stakeholders and prioritise relationships by mutual value potential.
- ✓ Invest in diverse networks to amplify learning and opportunity flow.
- ✓ Offer value first—information, introductions, or support—before seeking help.
- ✓ Collaborate through win-win projects that showcase shared success.
- ✓ Leverage digital platforms to extend visibility and credibility.
- ✓ Maintain relationship health with systematic touch-points and gratitude loops.

Reflection Question: Which single KPI will you review weekly to stay laser-focused on outcomes?

Integration Protocol –
A 90-Day Roadmap for Operationalizing the Five Pillars

Professional excellence is not an abstract ideal; it is a disciplined, repeatable process.

After mastering the five pillars of Authentic Presence, Communication Mastery, Growth Orientation, Results Driven Execution, and Strategic Connection, your next challenge is to turn your insights into clear, measurable results.

A 90-day sprint is long enough to create enduring change and short enough to sustain intensity. Treat the pages that follow as your field laboratory: you will benchmark your current performance, engineer SMART objectives, schedule high-frequency feedback loops, and harvest lessons learned. At Day 90 you will emerge with new capabilities, documented wins, and a playbook you can iterate indefinitely.

1. Baseline Diagnostics

Begin with a frank self-audit. For each pillar, select the statement that best mirrors your day-to-day behavior.

Pillar	Emerging (1)	Practicing (2)	Exemplary (3)
Authentic Presence	Values unclear; brand message inconsistent	Values articulated; behavior occasionally aligns	Values visible daily; trusted culture ambassador
Communication Mastery	Messages are often misunderstood; limited feedback loops	Clear messaging, practices active listening	Influential storyteller; adapts style to any audience
Growth Orientation	Learning ad-hoc avoids feedback	Maintains learning goals; seeks feedback periodically	Runs continuous experiments; feedback embedded in workflow
Results-Driven Execution	Goals are vague; progress is rarely tracked	Sets measurable objectives; reviews monthly	Drives OKRs; leads weekly KPI huddles; course-corrects early
Strategic Connection	Network limited to comfort zone	Cultivates cross-functional relationships	Builds diverse, reciprocal networks that unlock opportunities

Action: Sum your scores (maximum 15). Any pillar ≤ 2 becomes a priority focus for this sprint.

167

2. Objective Engineering

Turn your diagnostics into SMART goals: specific, measurable, achievable, relevant, and time bound. Focus on no more than three objectives to maintain strategic clarity.

SMART Goal Worksheet	
Goal Statement	e.g., *Increase stakeholder NPS from 42 → 55 by Q4.*
Key Metrics	Metric, baseline, target
Pillar(s) Activated	e.g., Communication Mastery; Strategic Connection
Why It Matters	Business impact & personal benefit

3. Execution Architecture

1. Decompose each SMART goal into bi-weekly deliverables.
2. Assign clear owners (even if that owner is you) and list supporting resources.
3. Map milestones on a Gantt chart or sprint calendar.
4. Identify leading indicators to monitor every week (not just lagging results).

4. High-Frequency Feedback Loop

Commit to a 30-minute review every Friday. Log wins, blockers, and next steps.

Week	Win(s)	Blockers	Adjustment / Next Step
1			
2			
3			
4			
5			

After 12 weeks, analyze patterns: Which habits delivered the greatest ROI? What obstacles recurred?

5. Post-Sprint Debrief

On Day 90 hold a structured debrief with a mentor or peer cohort.

Review:

- Outcomes vs objectives
- Unexpected insights and how they map to each pillar
- Systemic barriers that demand long-term fixes

Translate these findings into refined objectives for the next 90-day cycle.

Why This Protocol Works

- Temporal focus: Ninety days balances urgency with feasibility.
- Systems thinking: Weekly feedback loops prevent drift and enable rapid course correction.
- Compounding capability: Each sprint layers new skills onto a proven framework, accelerating professional growth.

Begin your Integration Protocol today, because sustained excellence is the product of deliberate cycles, not isolated achievements.

References

The following sources informed and supported the concepts, frameworks, and practical recommendations presented throughout The Professional Edge Playbook. They include foundational theories, contemporary research, and widely respected guides to professional practice.

1. Adler, R. B., Rosenfeld, L. B. & Proctor, R. F. (2019). Interplay: The Process of Interpersonal Communication. 14th ed. Oxford University Press.

2. Brown, B. (2018). Dare to Lead: Brave Work. Tough Conversations. Whole Hearts. Random House.

3. Buckingham, M. & Clifton, D. O. (2001). Now, Discover Your Strengths. Free Press.

4. Clampitt, P. G. (2016). Communicating for Managerial Effectiveness: Problems, Strategies, Solutions. 6th ed. Sage.

5. Covey, S. R. (2006). The Speed of Trust: The One Thing That Changes Everything. Free Press.

6. Drucker, P. F. (1999). Management Challenges for the 21st Century. HarperBusiness.

7. Duckworth, A. (2016). Grit: The Power of Passion and Perseverance. Scribner.

8. Eurich, T. (2018). Insight: The Surprising Truth About How Others See Us, How We See Ourselves, and Why the Answers Matter More Than We Think. Currency.

9. Gallo, C. (2014). Talk Like TED: The 9 Public-Speaking Secrets of the World's Top Minds. St. Martin's Press.

10. Harris, L. & Rae, A. (2011). Building a personal brand through social networking. Journal of Business Strategy, 32(5), pp.14–21.

11. Heath, C. & Heath, D. (2007). Made to Stick: Why Some Ideas Survive and Others Die. Random House.

12. Kaputa, C. (2012). You Are a Brand! How Smart People Brand Themselves for Business Success. 2nd ed. Nicholas Brealey Publishing.

13. Kolb, D. A. (1984). Experiential Learning: Experience as the Source of Learning and Development. Prentice Hall.

14. Labrecque, L. I., Markos, E. & Milne, G. R. (2011). Online personal branding: Processes, challenges, and implications. Journal of Interactive Marketing, 25(1), pp.37–50.

15. Lair, D. J., Sullivan, K. & Cheney, G. (2005). Marketization and the Recasting of the Professional Self. Management Communication Quarterly, 18(3), pp.307–343.

16. Mehrabian, A. (1972). Nonverbal Communication. Aldine-Atherton.

17. Montoya, P. & Vandehey, T. (2002). The Brand Called You: Make Your Business Stand Out in a Crowded Marketplace. McGraw-Hill.

18. Osterwalder, A. & Pigneur, Y. (2010). Business Model Generation. Wiley.

19. Pease, A. & Pease, B. (2004). The Definitive Book of Body Language. Bantam.

20. Peters, T. (1997). The brand called you. Fast Company, 10, pp.83–90.

21. Pink, D. H. (2009). Drive: The Surprising Truth About What Motivates Us. Riverhead Books.

22. Plain Language Action and Information Network (2011). Federal Plain Language Guidelines. U.S. Government.

23. Rampersad, H. K. (2008). Authentic Personal Branding: A New Blueprint for Building and Aligning a Powerful Leadership Brand. Information Age Publishing.

24. Schwartz, S. H. (2012). An overview of the Schwartz theory of basic values. Online Readings in Psychology and Culture, 2(1).

25. Shepherd, I. D. H. (2005). From cattle and coke to Charlie: Meeting the challenge of self marketing and personal branding. Journal of Marketing Management, 21(5–6), pp.589–606.

26. Van Dijck, J. (2013). The Culture of Connectivity: A Critical History of Social Media. Oxford University Press.

27. Adler, R. B., Rosenfeld, L. B., & Proctor, R. F. (2019). Interplay: The Process of Interpersonal Communication (14th ed.). Oxford University Press.

28. Baker, W. (2011). Achieving Success Through Social Capital: Tapping Hidden Resources in Your Personal and Business Networks. Jossey-Bass.

29. Brown, B. (2018). Dare to Lead: Brave Work. Tough Conversations. Whole Hearts. Random House.

30. Buckingham, M., & Clifton, D. O. (2001). Now, Discover Your Strengths. Free Press.

31. Clampitt, P. G. (2016). Communicating for Managerial Effectiveness (6th ed.). SAGE Publications.

32. Covey, S. R. (2006). The Speed of Trust: The One Thing That Changes Everything. Free Press.

33. Duckworth, A. (2016). Grit: The Power of Passion and Perseverance. Scribner.

34. Drucker, P. F. (1999). Management Challenges for the 21st Century. HarperBusiness.

35. Eurich, T. (2018). Insight: The Surprising Truth About How Others See Us, How We See Ourselves, and Why the Answers Matter More Than We Think. Currency.

36. Gallo, C. (2014). Talk Like TED: The 9 Public-Speaking Secrets of the World's Top Minds. St. Martin's Press.

37. Goleman, D. (2013). Focus: The Hidden Driver of Excellence. Harper.

38. Hackman, J. R. (2002). Leading Teams: Setting the Stage for Great Performances. Harvard Business Review Press.

39. Harris, L., & Rae, A. (2011). Building a personal brand through social networking. Journal of Business Strategy, 32(5), 14–21.

40. Heath, C., & Heath, D. (2007). Made to Stick: Why Some Ideas Survive and Others Die. Random House.

41. Kaputa, C. (2012). You Are a Brand! (2nd ed.). Nicholas Brealey Publishing.

42. Kolb, D. A. (1984). Experiential Learning: Experience as the Source of Learning and Development. Prentice Hall.

43. Labrecque, L. I., Markos, E., & Milne, G. R. (2011). Online personal branding: Processes, challenges, and implications. Journal of Interactive Marketing, 25(1), 37–50.

44. Lair, D. J., Sullivan, K., & Cheney, G. (2005). Marketization and the Recasting of the Professional Self. Management Communication Quarterly, 18(3), 307–343.

45. Mehrabian, A. (1972). Nonverbal Communication. Aldine-Atherton.

46. Montoya, P., & Vandehey, T. (2002). The Brand Called You: Make Your Business Stand Out in a Crowded Marketplace. McGraw-Hill.

47. Osterwalder, A., & Pigneur, Y. (2010). Business Model Generation: A Handbook for Visionaries, Game Changers, and Challengers. Wiley.

48. Pease, A., & Pease, B. (2004). The Definitive Book of Body Language. Bantam.

49. Peters, T. (1997). The brand called you. Fast Company, (10), 83–90.

50. Pink, D. H. (2009). Drive: The Surprising Truth About What Motivates Us. Riverhead Books.

51. Plain Language Action and Information Network (PLAIN). (2011). Federal Plain Language Guidelines. Retrieved from https://www.plainlanguage.gov/media/FederalPLGuidelines.pdf

52. Rampersad, H. K. (2008). Authentic Personal Branding: A New Blueprint for Building and Aligning a Powerful Leadership Brand. Information Age Publishing.

53. Rogers, C. R., & Farson, R. E. (1957). Active Listening. Industrial Relations Center of the University of Chicago.

54. Schwartz, S. H. (2012). An overview of the Schwartz theory of basic values. Online Readings in Psychology and Culture, 2(1). https://doi.org/10.9707/2307-0919.1116

55. Shepherd, I. D. H. (2005). From cattle and coke to Charlie: Meeting the challenge of self-marketing and personal branding. Journal of Marketing Management, 21(5–6), 589–606.

56. Van Dijck, J. (2013). The Culture of Connectivity: A Critical History of Social Media. Oxford University Press.

www.ingramcontent.com/pod-product-compliance
Lightning Source LLC
Chambersburg PA
CBHW052342210326
41597CB00037B/6223